THE JOURNEY TO MEANING

Creating the Business and Life of Your Dreams

BY DONALD F. HADLEY CFP, CHFC, MSM
with Curtis Verstraete

ISBN# 978-0-9731073-5-7

DEDICATIONS

This book is dedicated to everyone I have ever met, since I have become a composite of all of those people. Some have touched me in minor ways for just a moment and left an impression, while others have made a deeper mark. I carry the torch they have passed on to me and I endeavor to pass it on to future generations.

Specifically, I dedicate this book to my wonderful loving wife, Debra, who helps me daily to build the life and business of our dreams.

Also, to Rebecca and Laurel, who as critical parts of my core team are my Kevlar vest in fending off the "1000 ducks" of this world. They cause us to be the truly creative enterprise we are continually becoming.

To Curtis Verstraete, who breathed life into this project and demonstrated tremendous dignity and creativity while under the duress of being "Hadley'd".

To our children who motivate us as the ones to whom we will pass the torch.

To Nana and Grandad who never lost their excitement over the magnificent mystery of life and taught me so much about the world as it is and the world as it ought to be.

To my father who taught me such tremendous values.

To Bob DeMarco who first sent me to Korea.

To Dan Sullivan who sparked the re-engineering of our company so many years ago.

DEDICATIONS

To Bill Dix who is the best manager and teacher I have ever known.

To Bob Cogan for the dignity and integrity he has shown in allowing me to leave the "fold" and then come back again.

To all of our clients for continuously inspiring and financing our adventure.

To all of our suppliers who help us to become better through their expertise.

To all of the wonderful authors, writers and teachers, living and dead, that through the years have shared their wisdom and allowed us to work from such a strong base.

And, above all else to God, who originally created all of this...

TABLE OF CONTENTS

INTRODUCTION

I learned who I wanted to be and what I wanted to do with my life in the summer of 1980.

Up to that point, I thought playing sports and hanging out with my friends was pretty much what life was all about. I knew school was important to my parents so I did the work necessary to keep up my grades. Working at a job was something I had done here and there to earn pocket money. My vision of the future was a mixture of naïve and vague images that included driving an expensive car to a cool job in a modern building, and then coming home at the end of the day to a big house with a pool. Oh, and there was a wife, some kids and a dog in there somewhere.

My vision for my future became clear and very real over the course of two weeks in late August. It started one Monday morning, with my father asking me to meet him for lunch. We met in a restaurant near his office and after ordering, he asked me what I wanted to do with my life. I remember just staring at him. I didn't answer and my mouth may have been hanging open because he smiled and said, "That's what I thought your answer would be."

I didn't want to appear completely stupid, but I was grasping when I blurted out that I thought I would like to own my own business.

"Just like you do," I added.

Well, I didn't know it yet, but I had just opened a door that once I stepped through would shut behind me; there would be no turning back. (Actually, it's more accurate to say I stumbled through the door thanks to a healthy push from my father.)

My father told me that if I thought I was going to be a business owner, I had better start right away. He said the first thing I needed to do was figure out what being a business owner was really like. He then asked me to interview a dozen of his friends and acquaintances that were business owners. He told me to call them, introduce myself, tell them what I was up to and treat them to breakfast or lunch. He gave me eight questions to ask and said I should come up with four of my own. He didn't give me any money, so I knew the meals would come out of my pocket.

What I learned from the interviews changed my life. As soon as I got over the realization that my father was actually a pretty cool guy, I knew I wanted to be like the subjects of my interviews; they were real people. They were practical and knew what life was all about. Most revealing at the time was learning they measured success by the number of people they helped, the difference they made in the world, and by their ability to create greater meaning in their lives and in the lives of everyone around them. It wasn't just about money.

This revelation set me off on a journey of discovery, a lifelong search to learn what it takes to be a successful business owner.

Along the way, I have learned most business owners treasure independence above all else. I have also learned that the ones who are truly independent know they cannot succeed on their own. They rely on their customers, employees, suppliers, families and friends for the support, encouragement and understanding needed to succeed. They seek advice and guidance from experts and advisors who help them navigate new territory and address persistent problems.

I learned there is a circular dynamic at work here. In order to be truly independent as an individual, you need to be successfully interdependent as a business owner. And, in order to be successfully interdependent as a business owner, you need to be independent as an individual. When you don't create interdependency in your business, you cap its potential. It is limited by what you and you alone can do and your potential can diminish over time as you force yourself to do things outside of your natural talents. Passion wanes, burn-out sets in, and then you have no one but yourself to turn to for inspiration and energy.

So, where does it all begin and what sustains this circular dynamic?

Through all of the years I have helped business owners, I learned the single most powerful force behind their success is a clear, continuous and powerful conversation about what is most important to them. This conversation enables them to define the meaning of their life. This meaning gives their business focus and purpose, which in turn reinforces who they are and why they are here.

Although my journey is far from over, I have written this book to share what wisdom I have learned so far. My goal is to help you build a business that honors and nurtures your purpose, contributes to the well being of those around you, and helps you live a life filled with meaning.

Don Hadley March, 2008

About this book

To create this book, I have collaborated with Curtis Verstraete, one of the many people who have helped me develop and refine my business over the years. Curtis has been instrumental in the clarification and packaging of the principles, concepts, and strategies I use to help my clients. To produce this book, Curtis helped me refine the strategies and content for each chapter as well as write the action and dialogue sequences.

This book is written as a parable that follows friends on a wilderness adventure of discovery and growth. Richard and Michael are composites of the many people my team and I have met, worked with, and learned from throughout our careers and their journey is a metaphor for all the journeys taken by the many clients I have helped.

As their adventure unfolds, they explore important concepts and strategies for creating a life and business filled with meaning. To help you apply these strategies and concepts to your life and business, we have provided exercises at the end of each chapter. You can

INTRODUCTION

choose to read the book straight through and then go back to the exercises, or work through it chapter by chapter. Above all, I sincerely hope this book makes a contribution to your business, your life and your total overall success.

*(To download additional copies of these exercises, visit our web site www.ffgusa.com and enter this password: **Journey**).*

Chapter #1
The Meaningless Treadmill

"Stop acting as if life is a rehearsal. Live this day as if it were your last. The past is over and gone. The future is not guaranteed."
Wayne Dyer

My name is Michael and through thick and thin I have always thought of myself as an optimistic, positive person with the strength, intelligence, and, I guess, the courage to meet any challenge the world can throw at me.

I have proven my abilities time and time again as I built my business and lived my life. My business is all mine: I created it out of nothing, no one knows it better than I do, and no one can manage it like I can. I have always had the energy - a seemingly infinite source of power - to do what was necessary to make my business and my life a success.

If you were to take a snapshot today, the picture of my life would look pretty good. I have a great home, my family is very well provided for, and we live in the best neighborhood in town. My business is growing, my employees are well paid, and we constantly acquire new clients. To top it all off, here I was driving to meet my best friend for a week of rest and relaxation in one of the country's finest, unspoiled wilderness areas.

But, despite how great my life may look from the

outside, driving gave me time to think about my life, and the more I thought about it, the less successful I felt. In fact, I felt tired, desperate and confused.

My journey had begun just before dawn. But, by the time I completed the drive from my home in Spartanburg, South Carolina to my friend Richard's acreage, the sun had burned off the morning haze. Squinting as I turned into the tree-lined drive, I saw Richard standing on the front steps. As I got out of my car, he greeted me with a tremendous hug and then invited me into his kitchen for breakfast. He loves to cook and always makes a special meal whenever we get together. Thanks to the good food and his excitement for our trip, I was able to put aside my feelings and enjoy the moment.

After breakfast, I grabbed my bag from the car, and threw it in the back of his new Land Rover. Richard had made all the arrangements and told me to bring only my clothes and personal toiletries.

"Hey, where's all the stuff we're going to need?" I asked when I saw there was only one large backpack in the vehicle.

"Don't worry, it is all taken care of at the other end," Richard said. "The outfitter knows his business and I trust him."

We drove to the private landing strip where Richard kept his twin-engine airplane and we were in the air just before eight o'clock.

We were headed to the town of Ely in northern Minnesota and as we flew, I looked down and began worrying about not being prepared for the trip. I started to question Richard's faith in the outfitter, but realized I shouldn't worry because I trusted Richard. He had always said and done the right things, so why should I feel this way?

As we flew over the Blue Ridge Mountains, I kept telling myself life was great and I should feel great, but instead feelings of desperation and confusion again began to worry me. Above all, I felt very, very tired. All I could think about was the mess I would probably have to deal with when the trip was over. It was oppressive. My stomach began to sour and I began to dread what was ahead.

Just then, Richard tapped me on the shoulder and with a huge grin said, "Michael, do you read me? Come in Michael. Earth to Michael! It's a beautiful morning, you're with one of the greatest guys on the planet, so what's eating you?"

I couldn't help but smile, but I also needed to come clean. "Look Richard, I know we've been planning this trip for months, but I'm just not sure I should be leaving the business right now."

His grin turned to a gentle smile as he said, "I may be wrong, but I think you worry too much. After all, how many bad things could happen in a week?"

"Oh, don't ask," I said. "Just last week, my goofy brother-in-law landed a new account by promising to give them the world. Trouble is, he gave it to them for the price of Pennsylvania. No matter how often I tell him, he just can't seem to understand how to do things the right way.

"And then my accountant tells me our cash flow projections are way off so I had to dip into my personal account to make payroll. I hate doing that, it makes me feel like I'm going backwards.

"I barely see my wife and kids lately because I'm always at the office. I guess they are getting used to it because they don't seem to miss me any more.

"I feel like a slave to my business despite having hired some top notch people over the years. The business doesn't run perfectly unless I'm there. My employees just don't get it. No matter how often I tell them the right way to do things, they eventually go off the rails one way or another. They can't seem to make even the simplest of decisions on their own. And then, when things go wrong, no one takes responsibility and I'm left to clean up the mess. It's like they don't know why we are in business.

"I'm beginning to wonder about that too. Why am I in business? Why does it seem like I have less and less time to do what I like best? And I don't dare implement any new ideas... in fact, I can't remember the last time I had a good new idea. It's like I've forgotten why I started the business.

"And that's not all! Two weeks ago, I got a letter from my attorney that says one of our former employees has launched a lawsuit because they don't think they got the retirement benefits they were promised. I mean really! We have one of the best packages around, so what gives?

"To top it all off, I'm not sleeping at night. I wake up at all sorts of outrageous hours worried about what will happen next and stewing over whether or not it's all worth it. Everything I own is tied to the business. What if it fails? What if I'm wrong? I don't even know what the business is worth or how I'll ever be able to retire."

Even though I wanted to go on, I had to stop for a breath. Richard's eyes had widened with amazement while I ranted. When I stopped he managed to smile and glare at the same time. I had seen this look before: it meant, "You're going to do what I say and you're going to like it".

"Michael, answer this simple question: What progress have you made over the past year?"

The question was like an unwanted guest at dinner, it barged in on my self-pity and frustration and I knew it wouldn't go away until it was satisfied. As upset as I was, the fear and frustration I felt was familiar. Even though it wasn't comfortable, it was familiar and my infinite source of energy had enabled me to cope with it for a long time. In my eyes, I was a hero for coping with all the stuff thrown at me. I didn't want to feel good, I wanted someone to acknowledge how much of a sacrifice I was making day in and day out.

"Look Michael," Richard said after watching me struggle to answer. "Take it easy. Stop and take a breath, relax for a minute. Trust me, I can tell you need to step back and let things go. You're so focused on controlling everything you've lost your sense of direction."

He paused for a second and then with a huge grin said, "Based on the story you just told me, a week isn't going to make a difference because things couldn't possibly get any worse! And besides, you just never know who we might run into out there. Perhaps you'll bump into someone who'll help you see that your glass is more than half full."

Author's note

One of my favorite quotes comes from Lou Tice who said, "I turned my face for just a moment and ten years later it became my life".

The scorecard below will help you stop and do an accounting of your current situation. This type of assessment is critical if you are to break through the daily grind all business owners face and avoid looking up after a lifetime of effort only to wonder, "What happened, where did my life go?"

Worksheet #1: The Vision Builder Scorecard and Questionnaire

To help you clearly understand your current situation, try The Comprehensive Independence Scorecard. Rate your reactions to each pair of phrases. Decide where you lie on the scale from 1 to 10. Add up column totals to get your score. Speak to one of our coaches to understand the significance of your score.

I do not have clear personal goals and they are not written down		I have clear personal goals and they are written down
I do not have a plan in place for ensuring my children's financial and emotional independence		I have a plan in place for ensuring my children's financial and emotional independence
I do not have clear written business goals and strategies		I have very clear written business goals and strategies
I feel as if my business controls my life		I feel I am in control of my life and my business
I do not have the right people in the right places in my business		I have the right people in the right places in my business
My employees do not understand or buy into my vision for the future of the business		My employees understand and buy into my vision for the future of the business
I do not feel I am adequately compensated for the risk and time my business requires		I feel I am adequately compensated for the risk and time my business requires
I do not know how much my business is worth		I know how much my business is worth
I do not have a practical method in place for exiting my business		I have a practical method in place for exiting my business
I do not have as much confidence in my future as I would like		I have a strong sense of confidence about my future
ADD COLUMN TOTALS		**YOUR SCORE**

14

Worksheet #1: The Vision Builder Scorecard and Questionnaire

For each individual score, ask yourself "Why did I give myself that score?"

After you thoroughly examine why you've given yourself each score, ask yourself "What can I do to improve this score?" In answering this question, be generous with yourself and acknowledge the progress you have made and can build on. Also, recognize the strengths you have, strengths to be protected and enhanced.

Now, take some time to answer these open-ended questions. They will help you gain greater clarity about where you are now, what your most important goals are, your strengths, your weaknesses, and some key opportunities for moving forward.

1. What are your greatest concerns?

2. What do you like most about your current situation?

3. What needs to happen in the next three years for you to feel you were protecting and enhancing your business, improving your quality of life, and achieving your goals?

4. What significant progress have you made with developing your business?

5. What do you enjoy about your life now?

6. What progress have you already made towards achieving your goals?

7. What roadblocks stand in your way to achieving your goals listed in question 3?

8. What are the most important actions you must take to overcome the roadblocks listed in question 7?

9. What actions do you need to take first?

10. What actions will you take in the next 30 days?

CHAPTER #2
ONE MAN'S MEANING IS ANOTHER'S INSPIRATION

*"Most people go to their graves with their music
still inside them."*
Oliver Wendell Holmes

Richard flashed his winning smile at me and was about to say something else when he was interrupted. He held up a finger, as if to say "one minute" and began speaking "Roger Indianapolis, this is November, niner, seven, four, seven, Quebec…"

As he spoke to air traffic control I thought about how Richard is always on top of things. Although he is only a few years older than I am, he seems much wiser, calmer and in control. I often kid him about how calm and confident he is and how he always sees the best in people and the world around him.

"Hey Zen-man, sorry about that… I don't want to ruin things for you," I said after he finished.

"That's OK, I know what it's like," he said. He smiled as I raised my eyebrows. "I know you think I have it all figured out, but you know what, that isn't the case at all."

"There is so much I don't know, and so much more I want to do, and of course, there are all the mistakes I've made along the way. Believe me, I've been there. I know how it feels to wake up terrified in the middle of the night."

"About twenty years ago, I was in rough shape. My business was almost bankrupt, I was going through a messy – to say the least – divorce, and one afternoon when I was in my office, I lost it. My heart started pounding, I felt dizzy, I couldn't breathe, I thought I was about to die. The doctor couldn't find anything physically wrong with me and he said I most likely had suffered an anxiety attack.

"I knew I needed to do something to change the direction I was headed. I asked my accountant if he could recommend someone to help me sort out the mess in my business. He told me about a coaching organization that was helping one of his other clients re-organize their management team. I had nothing to lose, so I agreed to a meeting and my accountant set up a lunch for the three of us.

"That's how I met the person who has been coaching me ever since. For now, let me just call him the Coach. At the restaurant, my accountant introduced us and told him about some of the problems I was having. He listened carefully and then asked me a very simple question: Why do you own your business?

"You would think such a simple question would be easy to answer, but instead I froze. My mind raced through dozens of perfectly good reasons, yet I couldn't pin one down that didn't sound like a scripted cliché from some bad movie.

"The Coach admitted much later on that he was worried he was being too blunt in asking the question. It took a long time, but working out the answer had a profound effect on me. I really had to dig deep to come up with an answer that made sense, and more importantly, I had to work hard to come up with an answer that resonated in my heart; one that had meaning and truly spoke to who I am and what I stand for. And, it never actually ends; I'm still working on my answer every day."

"Back then I was in business to make money and I was learning a lesson Henry Ford learned decades ago when he said, 'A business that makes nothing but money is a poor business'."

"I have been working with the Coach ever since. His organization has developed an amazing process filled with innovative strategies to help business owners focus on three key areas. These areas are: protecting and enhancing their business, improving their quality of life, and achieving their most important goals. Which area comes first and how you actually go through their process depends on what is most important to you, and what you feel needs the most work."

"For me, it all began with trying to answer that simple question: Why *did* I own my business?"

As Richard again turned his attention to the radio, I tried to picture him in those earlier days. It was difficult to imagine he was once near financial and personal ruin. In my mind he was an ideal role model: the perfect picture of success and happiness. He built up a very successful construction company and sold it for top dollar a few years ago. He currently owns several auto service centers throughout South Carolina and has an excellent manager doing the lion's share of the day-to-day work. He owns three sailboats, two airplanes, and a fabulous chalet in Breckenridge, not to mention his acreage outside of Spartanburg. The characteristic I admire most is his sense of adventure and desire to try new things. He has the humility to realize he doesn't have all the answers and isn't shy about opening up to entirely new ways of thinking and being. I think he innately understands that learning comes from doing new things and not being afraid to look foolish or make mistakes.

I was reminded of our first trip together when we went to visit an old aunt of his who owned a hotel in Argentina. Richard only had a very basic plan of action: rent a car and figure it out from there. When we arrived, his aunt pointed us in the right direction – mostly I think to keep us out of serious trouble – but Richard insisted on keeping things flexible. "You never know what we'll come across and we need to be ready for whatever happens," he told me while sitting in the dining room of his aunt's hotel.

We roamed the country for five days and we saw and experienced things I would never have seen or done on my own. And, we made it home in one piece with priceless memories and stories.

"Care to share the joke?" Richard asked. He had caught me smiling as I reminisced about our Argentinean adventure.

"If you have the answer to why you're in business, why do you do everything you can to stay away from your business?" I asked. "Well, that's funny," he said. "When I first started working with the Coach, he helped me understand that by focusing on what is absolutely most important to me, I would unlock the wisdom I needed to create greater vision and meaning."

"You're not answering my question," I said. "What does focusing on car service and repair have to do with vision and meaning?"

"Patience grasshopper," he chided with an ironic smile. "Let your guru speak and you will see the light."

"When I first began my construction company it was all about making money. As I said, that only got me so far. With the Coach's help I realized the most important thing in my life is to be able to make a difference in the lives of the people I care about. By focusing on what is most important to me, I saw quite clearly that the construction company was taking up far too much of my time, effort and energy. In fact it was causing me to be a burden to my wife, family, and even my employees. This new focus gave me the motivation to acquire and seek out the wisdom I needed to free myself from the day-to-day minutiae that weighs down most business owners."

I thought I had Richard in a corner. He still hadn't told me what was so meaningful about changing oil and selling tires, so I said, "And you're bringing enlightenment and meaning to car owners across South Carolina?"

"Look, I didn't pack a parachute for you, so you're stuck with me for at least another three hours. Early on in my work with the Coach, I was skeptical... no, I was cynical about his principles for unlocking wisdom to create greater vision and meaning. After all, what is the deeper meaning of building sewage plants and public utility buildings?"

"But, during our first working meeting, the Coach asked me to list 100 things I wanted to do in my lifetime. At the time I struggled to come up with a dozen and almost all of these focused on my family and my friends. It came to me slowly, but thanks to identifying my most important goals, I realized I alone had the power to define what was meaningful to me. And, as I dug deeper, I realized freedom was the ultimate goal, the most meaningful accomplishment I could ever dream of achieving."

"Well, it may sound too simple, but the realization that I was in business to create freedom for myself was like a turbocharger. It gave me an incredible boost of energy and, with the Coach's help, I was able to focus my energy on what I needed to do to achieve complete freedom."

"OK, OK, I think I get it," I said. "Your businesses – the construction company and now your auto service centers – make it possible for you to do what you want."

"That's it exactly," Richard said.

"At first this was difficult to do, but as I kept at it over the next few months things became much clearer.

This 100 goals exercise, and other methods the Coach uses, helped me define my unique talent, focus my efforts and achieve much greater personal results."

"He helped me assess the team I had built and I soon realized I was hiring people who were like me. I saw that because they shared my talents and weaknesses, we actually didn't make much of a team. Over the next year or so, the Coach helped me build a much more diverse team. And, because of its diversity, my team was much better able to leverage each others' efforts and the resources we had available to us."

"It didn't take long before the business could practically run itself thanks to the systems we set up for managing accountability, and the strategies we implemented that drove continuous improvement. At this point, the Coach said his job was to help me create, acknowledge, and nurture interdependence in my team so we could achieve greater business results and I could achieve the kind of personal freedom that had been eluding me."

"As it turned out, reorganizing the business so that it ran without my direct involvement made it a better business all around. We built a real company, not just a very complex and stressful job for me."

Richard was once again interrupted by ground control and he shifted back to flying and navigating with ease. I couldn't help but admire how in command he was. He was relaxed, alert, and totally in his element. He was completely free.

The Journey to Meaning

When you face your darkest times, when the challenges, problems and fear pile up it is always good to remember what Sumner Redstone said, "Success is not built on success. It's built on failure. It's built on frustration. Sometimes it's built on catastrophe."

In part, this means that companies that are consistently good never have to be great. Many times, being great comes from the need to be the very best, and merely good companies do not take the risks or go to the extremes greatness requires. If you have a powerful vision and tremendous dreams for the future, you will be able to learn from your mistakes, failures, and even from catastrophe.

Worksheet #2: 100 Things to Do Before I Die

Step #1: Think back to when you were growing up. What were your childhood dreams? What did you dream about becoming while you were in high school? College? When you started your business? What have you read about recently that you would like to try? What stories have you heard from other people that have you excited about learning a new skill or having a new experience?

Step #2: Make a list of everything you would like to learn, do, experience or try in your life.

Step #3: Match the items on your list with the different categories provided. Try and find some balance by having all areas of your life represented.

Step #4: Develop your priorities by setting dates based on what you think you can do and when you can get it done by.

Worksheet #2: 100 Things to Do Before I Die

Name: _____   Date: _____

To Do's: Category: Date To Do:

_____

_____

_____

_____

_____

_____

_____

_____

_____

_____

_____

_____

_____

_____

_____

_____

_____

_____

P = Personal   (Spiritual, Mental, Physical/Health, Emotional)
FM = Family
FR = Friends
B = Business
T = Travel
$ = Financial   Improving your results:
F/T = Fun or Toys   Share with your significant other.
L = Leadership   Share with friends.
C = Community   Share with your core team in your business.

CHAPTER #3
GETTING STARTED - ALL OVER AGAIN

"We need to set our course by the stars, not by the light of every passing ship."
Omar Bradley

After listening to Richard talk about his past, I was feeling a little more optimistic about my situation. I decided to relax, enjoy the view and just go along for the ride. Before long, exhaustion took over and, soothed by the droning of the engines, I fell into a deep, dreamless sleep.

I awoke to the sound of Richard singing a song I recognized from a tourism video I'd seen about our destination, something about silver waters at the end of the road. He didn't seem to know what the lyrics were, and he wasn't much at carrying a tune either.

"Hey Zen man... are you OK? You sound like your stomach hurts."

"I see a couple hours of sleep hasn't changed your sunny personality," Richard replied flashing a wide grin.

We were crossing the western tip of Lake Superior, a massive body of water that stretched eastward to the horizon. As we approached Ely, I was amazed by how many small lakes dotted the landscape. It seemed as if the land was floating in a vast basin, like a sponge that would sink if it absorbed even the least bit more water.

A modest landing strip next to three hangars, some office buildings and a café located a few miles south of town make up the Ely Municipal Airport. As we taxied to one of the hangars, a large, four-wheel drive truck came around the corner. The driver waved as he hopped out of the truck. He seemed very eager to greet us and as I climbed out of the plane, he was instantly beside me.

"Hey, you must be Michael," he said as he reached out to shake my hand. "I'm Mark Mazierski owner of Big Moose Outfitters."

My hand all but disappeared into his as he pumped it enthusiastically, smiling from ear to ear. "My friends call me Moose, and I am sure glad to meet you."

"Well," I stammered a bit. "It's great to meet you too Mark, ah... Moose."

"There, now we're friends," he said as he turned to greet Richard.

"Are you ready to get on the water?" Moose asked. "They say the weather is supposed to hold for the next four or five days, so you guys are in for some fine canoeing."

Richard smiled and said, "Moose, it's good to meet you in person. I think Michael and I are all set and we're in your hands."

We loaded our bags into the truck and Moose talked continuously as he drove us through town and then turned west along Shagawa Lake to Schaefer Bay. In the short time it took to reach his compound, Moose gave us a quick history of how he started his business, a review of the canoeing season so far, a story about a family that was lost for three days, and the details of the area we were heading into.

"Ely is known as the home of the Boundary Waters Canoe Area," he explained. "It's made up of one million acres of forest, lakes, rivers and streams and it's all part of the Superior National Forest. The Canadian border marks the northern edge and it is the largest wilderness preserve east of the Rockies. You know, there are over 1,500 miles of canoe routes and about 2,000 campsites out there."

"What about bears?" I asked. "I mean how many bears are out there?"

Moose laughed. "If you ask me, there are more bears hanging around town than out there," he said. "It's really only a few bad actors who are just getting lazy. They get a taste for people food and forget about everything else. It's like they don't appreciate how great it is out in the wild. No cars, no humans, no wardens with tranquilizer guns: sure they have to work a bit harder for their food out there, but to me it's got to be worth it."

"It's ironic," I said. "The bears are moving into town and we're moving into the wilderness. Maybe we should set up a time share agreement with them."

Richard and Moose were laughing as we pulled into the outfitter's compound: a tidy set-up tucked in the back of the bay. The compound's focal point is a large dock with room for several boats. Behind the dock, two racks of canoes and a freshly painted shed – which I soon learned was full of gear – lent the scene a very business-like appearance.

As Moose jumped out of the truck he said, "Come up to the house and we'll get the paperwork finished and get you guys on your way."

We followed him to a large chalet about 200 feet from the shore. Although it looked rustic, it was in perfect condition and nothing seemed out of place.

"I've got your entry permits ready," Moose said. "It's a good thing you called when you did, permits are given out on a quota basis and there were only a few left for the entry point and route you wanted."

The paper work went quickly and Moose led us out to the dock. "OK, let's see what we've got here," he said. "You need to cover a lot of ground, I mean water, to start, so we've set up two canoes and an engine for you. The rest of it is pretty standard…"

"Whoa," I said. "Two canoes and a motor, what are you talking about?"

"Don't worry Michael," Richard said. Moose had looked at me with surprise when I spoke and then looked to Richard for help.

"The motor is too big for one canoe and we will need it to cover some open water quickly. It's only to get us started and then we will separate the canoes and paddle the rest of the way."

Richard and Moose seemed to think everything was perfectly normal, so I went along and tried to help load the canoes.

GETTING STARTED - ALL OVER AGAIN

"My pack is waterproof," Richard told me, "and I recommend you get one from Moose for your stuff."

"I don't have one around for you to borrow, sorry about that," Moose apologized. "I can sell you a new one and you can settle up with me when you get back."

My idyllic vision of the trip was marred by my lack of preparation and the thought of using an outboard motor for the first day. It wasn't what I expected but there was nothing I could do about it. I began to wonder why I was taking the trip and the feelings I had earlier in the morning came rushing back, replacing the sense of anticipation I had enjoyed since waking from my nap.

"Richard, are you sure about this motor thing?"

"Don't worry, it'll be worth it, you'll see."

Richard was busy getting everything squared away and didn't have time to worry about my doubts. Soon, we were on our way. I sat in the rear of one of the canoes while Richard, seated in the other, handled the tiller of the nine-horse power engine.

Even though we were moving quickly, I was irritated because I really wanted to paddle. I had hoped to exorcise my demons, or at least forget about them for a while, by exercising my body. It wasn't happening: despite the rush of being on the water and the spectacular scenery, my worries about the business, my future, my family, and everything else forced their way into my mind. I was miserable.

It took almost four hours for us to reach our first

campsite. We had to cross the western third of Shaga-wa Lake, travel up a winding river to Burntside Lake and go across open water north to Long Island.

Richard hadn't said a word the entire time. He seemed very content to simply take care of what need-ed to be done in order to get us to our destination.

As we were unloading our gear, Richard put his hand on my shoulder to stop me. "So, what's eating you?" he asked.

"Well, motoring for four hours, not saying a word, ringing ears, the taste of gasoline in my mouth... oth-er than that, welcome to the great outdoors, it's all great."

"Look," Richard said. I could tell he was debating how to handle my peevishness. I expected to get a blast of anger but instead he said, "Look Michael, I planned this trip in detail with Moose's help. He's an expert who can tell you in five minutes stuff that would take you five years to learn on your own. I shared the vi-sion you and I had of the trip, what we wanted to do, how long we wanted to be away, what we wanted to see, and he put together the best possible package he could."

"You've got to trust his expertise and relax. Even though you think we started off on the wrong foot, we've made a great start."

"I guess you're right," I said. "It's just that I spent the last four hours worrying about my business and everything else. Not my idea of fun."

"Well now we've got time to talk about it," Richard said as he began gathering kindling. "Let me tell you more about the Coach I work with."

"I remember how he helped me develop a very clear and meaningful vision for my life. He began by having me look at where I had been: my childhood lessons, the influence my parents had, my accomplishments, and my failures were examined and assessed for how they shape my personality and approach to what the world throws at me."

"That sounds pretty deep," I said. "How did the Coach get you to open up so much?"

"It took a little time, but he seemed to always know when to ask questions and when to listen. He helped me see I had forgotten or discarded many valuable lessons I had already learned. I had forgotten a lot of the wisdom I had accumulated."

"The Coach used a 20 question exercise to help me see my life from a new perspective. The answers to his questions made me look back and recognize the patterns in my life. What was most exciting was the realization that there was a formula to my past successes, a pattern I could learn to repeat when necessary."

"I also learned I was more tied to my parents than I realized. I carry baggage that shows up in how I relate to the people who are most important to me and my success."

"What do you mean?" I asked.

"Well, sparing all the gory details, let's just say I had a lot of issues around trust and intimacy. I used to only let people see the surface and never let them see the real me. It's because of the story I used to have in my head about not being good enough. This made me compensate by trying to be better than everyone around me. I was a bit of a bully and pushed people away when they tried to help."

"Man, that doesn't sound like you at all!"

"No, I guess it doesn't. But, it was me and the Coach helped me recognize and accept it."

"That doesn't sound right," I said. "I would expect you to try to change it, not accept it."

"It does sound backward, but I learned that accepting who I was made it easier for me to accept other people for who they are. This was the beginning of a profound change for me. I constantly review my progress to assess where I am, and what my thoughts and feelings are about each day."

"This then gives me the clarity I need to see where I want to go, and what I want to do. You know, this trip is a good analogy for what I have learned. Imagine we wanted to get to the Northwoods but didn't know where we were. It would be hopeless: you can't navigate if you don't know where you are."

"Well, that sounds too simple," I grumbled. I still felt put out by how our journey had begun. "Everyone knows you can't get somewhere if you don't know where you're starting from."

"You're right," Richard answered, raising his hands in a conciliatory gesture. "But think about how the two concepts work together: your life vision coupled with an honest, ongoing appraisal of where you are. It creates a dynamic navigation system for your life."

"If you say so," was all I could think of in reply.

We busied ourselves preparing for night as the sun was rapidly setting. We had a simple dinner of freeze-dried soup and a sandwich. We ate quickly and doused the fire.

Just as I was crawling into my tent, Richard said, "Michael, I know you're going through a rough time, and I know you are not happy with how our trip has started, but do me – and yourself – a small favor. Think about how excited we were all those nights we planned this trip. Think about the wilderness you have been craving and the peace it promises. Go to sleep with your vision in your head and let's just see what happens tomorrow."

Author's note

There are many ways to develop a clear meaningful vision for your life. What is constant throughout is that it takes work and, above all, honesty. And, it is a job that is never done. Accept this fact and keep at it for your entire life.

"Peace comes not from the absence of conflict, but from the ability to cope with it."
Don Millman

Worksheet #3: Your Personal Vision

Step #1: Review your worksheets from Chapters #1 and #2.

Step #2: Summarize your "100 things to do" into 5-10 overall lifetime goals.

Step #3: Is there a theme to your goals? Complete a first draft of why you are on this earth.

Step #4: What are you best at? What are 3-4 things you do in business and in your personal life that bring value to other people?

Step #5: List your 7 most important personal values.

(Remember, if you need extra worksheets, visit our web site @ www.ffgusa.com)

What Are Your Lifetime Goals?

_____

_____

_____

_____

_____

Why Are You On This Earth?

_____

_____

_____

_____

_____

What Are You Best At?

_____

_____

_____

_____

Worksheet #3: Your Personal Vision

_____

_____

What are your Guiding Principles or Values?

_____

_____

_____

_____

_____

Improving your results:

Have your spouse do this exercise and then share your answers with each other.

Give an example of each of your values in action and talk about it at the dinner table.

Get your family involved in this worksheet.

Do a similar worksheet with the core team in your business.

This worksheet will examine:

- Purpose - why you are in business
- Mission - what you are best at
- Vision - your long term goals
- Values - the values and principles that guide your company

CHAPTER #4
THE NATURE OF SETTING GOALS

*"Setting a goal is not the main thing. It is deciding
how you will go about achieving it and
staying with that plan."*
Tom Landry

As I lay in my tent, I felt out of place. After spending endless months immersed in my "real" life, to be abruptly camping out in the middle of nowhere was disconcerting.

My hearing sharpened as the ringing in my ears left over from the airplane and outboard engine slowly faded. I became increasingly aware of the steady gurgle and chuckle of water lapping against the rocky shore mixed with the rattle of leaves roused by gentle gusts of wind. I felt I was listening to a sound track playing just outside of the tent's nylon walls.

I smiled as I thought about a CD my wife recently bought, one of those cheesy meditation discs featuring the sounds of nature. Here I was listening to the real thing all the while feeling like I'm back home with my headset on.

My wife and I had quarreled two days before the canoe trip. When I told her I wasn't sure if I should go on the trip, she sighed and asked me what the point of going was if I didn't plan to enjoy myself. Trying to make her feel better, I said it would be great if we did something like this with the kids. She didn't seem to think I was serious and besides, she said, every time we go somewhere, I end up dealing with one business emergency or another. I told her it was not my fault and besides, the business made it possible for us to live like we do.

She just looked at me and said "Yeah... like we do."

The next morning I awoke to the smell of bacon frying. The bright sunshine cast sharply defined shadows of leaves on the walls of my tent. Richard was trying to sing that same tourism board song,

As I crawled out of the tent I said, "Oh, it's you, I thought some poor animal must have caught its leg in a trap."

Richard, ignoring my dig, said, "It's about time you got up. We've got a lot of ground to cover if we are going to get to our next camp site before dark."

As we ate breakfast, Richard asked, "Did you sleep in because you were dreaming about the perfect canoe trip?"

"No, not exactly. I was thinking about how fast-paced life is out there in the 'real' world. We never have time to slow down and enjoy where we are."

"I know what you mean," Richard said. "Modern life, especially for business owners, can seem like an endless stream of demands. We are constantly being asked for more of our time, our energy, passion, our ideas, patience, money and anything else we can give. You know, when you think about it, this trip makes a good analogy for what I've learned about meeting those demands."

"What do you mean?" I asked.

"Well, when I asked you to think about how we had envisioned what this trip would be like, I was trying to set you on a course for achieving the goals you said were absolutely necessary."

I didn't say anything, but Richard read my thoughts.

"OK, it's not a lecture, I just want you to compare how we planned this trip to how you are managing your business. You are successful, you've said so yourself, but you're also frustrated. And yesterday, you were upset because the trip didn't start off the way you wanted. Yet, when we did our planning, we set a specific goal of camping right here the first night and the only way to make it was to use the motor."

"That's the key to the success I know this trip is going to be," Richard continued. "We have set specific goals and we will measure our progress by reaching the camp sites we've agreed to."

"Now, based on my experience, the outfitter's advice, and your need to paddle until you drop, I know our goals are realistic in the time we have."

"So what's all this got to do with my business," I asked, immediately regretting the question as Richard's grin told me I had fallen into his trap.

"Come on, let's start packing up and I'll tell you."

As we unlashed the canoes and hid the outboard engine and one of the canoes in the bush Richard said, "You may have missed it, but the goals I just described are smart goals."

"Well, how smart can they be, they're just our travel plans."

"No, I mean smart goals as in the acronym SMART. That means they are Specific, Measurable, Agreed to, Realistic, and have a Time frame."

"OK... again, how does this relate to my business?"

"Well, let's use a real life example. What is one of your most important goals for this year?"

I was tempted to tell Richard to drop it. We were loading the last few things into the canoe and I just wanted to get on with the trip. When I didn't answer immediately, he didn't say anything and went on with the work.

Soon, everything was ready and I carefully got into the front of the canoe. Richard pushed off and we glided effortlessly into the mirror smooth lake. I instantly felt a deep sensation of being drawn forward by the water. I waited a moment before putting my oar in the water and felt as if the water alone was able to pull us towards our destination.

"Now, this is more like it," I said as I slipped my paddle into the water and pulled through a long, slow stroke.

We paddled for more than an hour without speaking. I was enjoying the exercise and the awesome scenery. We saw two other parties: a group of six people in three canoes and shortly afterwards, another twosome in a single canoe. A polite wave of the hand

and a nod of the head was the only interaction that felt appropriate.

"I guess my most important goal for this year is to grow the business by 20%," I said, finally addressing Richard's question.

He didn't respond so I asked, "20% is certainly attainable don't you think?"

"Michael, your goals need to be very specific," Richard said. "Vague goals that can't be measured are an invitation to procrastination because it is hard to know how to start working on them. What exactly does 20% mean? Is it net profit, gross sales, the number of new clients or something else entirely?"

"Um, gross sales," I said.

"OK, that's a good start. Now tell me who, what, why, when and how you are going to go about achieving this goal?"

"Specifics huh. Well, I'm going to do whatever it takes to find the new business and grow the existing accounts. My team is going to do most of the rest. What we do is pretty clear; we'll just do it better. When, well that's easy too, every day is when. How, same thing as what, we'll do it how we've always done it."

I thought this was a pretty good answer until Richard asked, "Why? You forgot about the why."

"Why not," I said turning to smile so he knew I realized he had once again cornered me. "Why indeed? Well, because if we don't grow, we'll get stale and may even go backwards. Why? Because I need to always be moving forward, looking for new ways to do business, new types of opportunities. Growth is really just a by-product of making the business better."

"OK, that's more like it," Richard said. "But you need to go back and get clear about the other elements of your goal. We know what your role will be but not how you will achieve your goal. How are you going to acquire new clients? What sorts of services and products will you use to grow your existing accounts?"

"Well, that's a lot of work, too much work for a canoe trip."

"Yep, it's a lot of work," Richard acknowledged. "That's why so many business owners don't do it and that's why so many find themselves working in a very stressful job instead of working on a very successful business."

We paddled for a while before I said, "S is for Specific. I get it, what does M stand for?"

"Measurable," Richard said. "If you are going to increase gross sales by 20% you will need to identify how you will measure your progress. For example, how many new clients do you think you need?"

"Well, it all depends on what size they are but if I average them out, I guess I would need at least 15."

"Good, now how many prospects will you have to approach in order to convert 15 of them into clients?"

"Sheesh, I don't know, I haven't really paid attention to that sort of thing."

"That's OK," Richard said. "Just give me your best guess."

"Does 150 prospects sound good?"

"We'll see," he replied. "That means you will need to get in front of 12 or more each month. What strategies do you have in place to make that happen?"

"Man, this is tough. Do you mean to tell me you've done all this thinking for your business?"

"Well, I never did, but the Coach has really made a big difference. He makes it easier to do this sort of thinking because he knows how to get me going and how to help me when I hit a roadblock."

"OK, I guess I like where this is going," I said. "But I don't really want to spend all day talking about my business. This scenery is just too awesome and besides, I think we need to stop for lunch."

We pulled up on a nearby shore and unloaded one of the purpose-built tubs Moose had provided. Richard unpacked a large coil of garlic sausage and some pita pockets. We quickly cut up the sausage, stuffed it into the pockets and added a little mustard.

"This is for sure the very best sandwich I've tasted in a long time," I said as I downed my first bite with a swig of bottled water.

Richard bit off a huge mouthful of his pita, puffed out his cheeks and gave me a goofy bug-eyed look.

"I'm almost afraid to ask, but the A in SMART, what's it stand for?

Richard swallowed, and wiping his mouth with the back of his hand said, "Agreed to."

"How does that work? I set the goals, the team does what's needed... at least that's supposed to be what happens."

"Well, how is it working? You said yourself that they never seem to make a decision for themselves. Worse, you said they never take responsibility when something goes wrong."

"Yeah, OK, so maybe they need to agree to something, but what is it?" I heard something in my voice I didn't like, I was beginning to whine.

"Like I said, it's not always that easy to think these things through," Richard said. "The good thing about it though is you get better at it over time, and once you start, you build on your progress and your team gets used to it too."

We cleaned up, reloaded the tub and were back on the water in a matter of minutes.

After paddling for a while I stopped and looked back over my shoulder. Richard was paddling smoothly, lost in his thoughts when I said, "That 'Agreed to' strategy is a toughie. Let's move on to R. What was R again?"

"Realistic," Richard replied. "Your goals have to be manageable in the time frame and with the current resources at your disposal. There is no point in creating a goal that requires resources that are unavailable or cannot be made available. And, speaking of 'Agreed to' you may need a brainstorming session with your team to find solutions to resource shortages. It's this type of thing that can empower your staff to help find new alternatives when resources are at a premium."

"Got it. Let's get to the T... time frame right?

"Right."

"That seems to be the simplest part of having SMART goals," I said.

"For the most part you're right. But, and this is important, if you cannot assign a deadline within your goal statement, you probably need to make your goal more specific. Assigning a finishing date allows you to go back and create benchmarks along the way to ensure that progress towards your goal is on schedule."

I let this sink in as we paddled along. I could see I had only a vague set of goals under the broad heading of "owning a successful business". It is natural for me to simply jump in and do what was needed to address the challenges each day threw at us. Longer term, structured goals, especially goals articulated in detail with the participation of my team, well, that would be something new to try.

"We're here," Richard said, interrupting my thoughts. "This is where we walk."

Our first portage was just under a mile long. After a quarter mile of climbing steadily, we found ourselves 150 feet above the lake looking out at a stunning, panoramic view of the wilderness.

"Man, oh man," I said. "This is a vision: I can see for miles. If I knew where to look, I could probably see our next couple of camp sites."

"Let's take a break," Richard said.

We put the canoe down and shucked off our packs. I sat down on a nearby rock and let my eyes wander across the horizon. The view was as perfect a picture as you can imagine. It looked like an artist's study in green: tall pines mixed with aspen, birch and poplar covered the hills and created a multi-hued blanket of infinite variety and natural harmony.

"Zen Man," I said, turning towards Richard, "If I had known how beautiful this was going to be, I wouldn't have given yesterday's motorized malarkey a second thought."

"You know, you're on to something there," he replied. "If I had done a better job of learning what your preferences and expectations were, instead of assuming you would go along because I was the 'leader' of this trip, I would have known about your distaste for the outboard."

"Oh, I like outboards well enough, but I expected we would hop in a canoe and paddle right from the start."

"This reminds me of how I used to be with my managers and employees," Richard went on. "I had the vision, the experience, the capital, and all they had to do was what I told them. And sometimes, they just had to do what I expected of them, as if they could read my mind."

I was actually getting into the conversation. Distracting as it was from the scenery, I was seeing very clearly how I was currently running my business.

"You know, I appreciate what you just said," I told Richard. "Not just in reference to this trip, but you've hit the nail on the head: I have been expecting my employees to read my mind. Just because it is obvious to me what needs to be done, I assume it should be obvious to them. Worse yet, I assume that what motivates me is incentive enough for them. But our expectations are not in alignment and it's no wonder we've been paddling in circles."

Worksheet #4, Step 1: Design an Overall Department/Division Goal

Complete A-G before going on to step 2.

A. Review Company/Division Purpose, Mission, Values and Long Term Vision.

B. What will your Department/Division look like in that Vision?

_____

_____

_____

_____

C. Draft # 1 of SMART Overall Goal for your Department/Division:

_____

_____

_____

_____

D. Share Draft #1 (item C above) with at least 3 other members of your core team to get feedback.

E. Draft #2 of SMART Overall Goal for your Department/Division:

_____

_____

_____

_____

F. Review Company/Division Purpose, Mission, Values and Long Term Vision. Does your Overall Department/Division Goal align with them?

G. Final Draft of SMART Overall Goal for your Department/Division:

_____

_____

_____

_____

Worksheet #4, Step 2: Identify Your Critical Success

Begin by listing all the obstacles you face and opportunities to be taken advantage of. Next, identify the strategies you will use to do so.

Step 2A: Step 2B:
Obstacles/Opportunities   Strategy

1._____   _____

2._____   _____

3._____   _____

4._____   _____

5._____   _____

6._____   _____

7._____   _____

8._____   _____

9._____   _____

10._____   _____

11._____   _____

12._____   _____

Worksheet #4, Step 2: Identify Your Critical Success

Review your results from 2A and 2B and identify the 5 most important factors that will be critical to your success. Refine the strategies you will use as needed.

Critical Success Factors (top 5 only)	Strategy
1._____	_____
2._____	_____
3._____	_____
4._____	_____
5._____	_____

2D: Share this with at least 3 other core team members:

- Are you missing any obstacles or opportunities?
- Are there any other potential tactical fixes?
- Who else do you need to talk with?
- Are the strategies highly impacting on the vision, cost effective and have good odds of success?

Worksheet #4, Step 3 The Strategy and Actions Connector

SMART Goal: _____

Transfer the 5 Strategies from Step 2 into the chart below in the left hand box, then complete the actions timeline.

Strategy	__/__/__ (5 Years)	__/__/__ (3 Years)	__/__/__ (1 Year)	__/__/__ (3 Months)	__/__/__ (1 Month)	__/__/__ (1 Week)	__/__/__ (1 Day)

Worksheet #4, Step 4: Resources Determination

Review your results in step 3 and identify the resources you will need to implement your plan and achieve your goals.

√	Resource	Details
	People	
	New Skills	
	Adjusted Attitudes	
	Existing Habits	
	New Habits	
	Structure	
	Software/Hardware/Equipment	
	Opportunities	
	Communication	
	Affirmations	

CHAPTER #5
MENDING ONE'S WAYS

"A poor carpenter blames his tools."
Anonymous

It was time to get moving so we had a quick snack of energy bars and water, picked up the packs and the canoe, and headed downhill towards our next launching point.

The work was strenuous as we maneuvered the canoe made heavy by gear lashed to the thwarts. I was thinking about the latest deal my brother-in-law had brought in. It was rife with problems; not least of which was we would lose money if we delivered everything he had promised. Had I been expecting him to read my mind? Did I not do a good enough job communicating with him? Did I even train him properly? Did I expect too much of him and at the same time did I fail to provide the support and the systems required to avoid issues like the ones we now faced?

It is difficult to navigate a steep footpath while carrying a heavy pack with your head stuck inside the back end of a 20-foot canoe. It is even more difficult when you pay more attention to the questions in your head than the world around you. A large moss-covered stone wedged between two pine roots was my undoing. As soon as I stepped on it, my feet went out from under me. My butt and the stern of the canoe hit the ground at the same time. I bounced on my backpack and rolled out from under the canoe just in time to see Richard trip forward, and then, grabbing a tree, stop the canoe from rolling any further down the steep hill.

"Was it something I said?" Richard asked calmly once he realized I wasn't hurt. The amused glint in his eyes told me I was going to catch a few more wise cracks before he let this one go.

"I guess I better let up on you if this is how you're going to take it," Richard continued, enjoying the moment while surveying for any damage to the canoe and our gear.

"Well, it is all your fault," I said with exaggerated sarcasm. "If you hadn't made me think about so much stuff, maybe I could focus on what I was doing."

"Here, drop your pack and let's get this canoe to the bottom of this hill. I can see a clearing down there where we can sort things out."

I shucked off my backpack and helped Richard get the canoe to the bottom of the hill. As we walked back up to retrieve the backpacks, Richard said, "So, I've got you thinking so much your mind is somewhere else. That's too bad. I'm sorry to distract you from enjoying this beautiful place."

"Well, I was thinking about all the things that aren't working in my business. The mess my brother-in-law made is just the tip of the iceberg. When I look back over all the years, I have tried to develop systems and processes to make the business run smoother. But, no matter what I do, there is always something or someone that doesn't quite fit."

"I know what you mean," Richard said, helping me take my backpack off. "I didn't know where to begin when I first realized I had to change the way I was thinking about and running my business."

"At first, I had to deal with a lot of guilt. I felt as if I had failed in many ways, and had been unfair to everyone who was trying to help me despite myself. I also felt ashamed and didn't want to admit I had been anything less than perfect. But, the Coach helped me realize the first step was coming clean with myself, and with anyone I truly wanted working with me."

"That's big," I said. "How did you get started? I mean how did you do break the news to your employees?"

"Well, it wasn't all that bad, once I realized I had to change my stripes. I needed to get back to basics and clarify what was most important to me. I was afraid to look that deeply, but with the Coach's help, I was able to come up with a very simple, powerful reason for making my business as good as it could be."

"I brought this vision to my team and asked each of them to see if it fit their own purpose. I asked them if they could see themselves playing a part in this vision. Most importantly, I asked each of them to figure out what their personal vision was, and to see where it intersected with mine. If we could all work together towards a shared vision, one that made our personal goals possible, we would have a team that couldn't be stopped."

I had to let this sink in. I felt a growing fear rise in my gut as I thought about coming clean with my employees, especially my brother-in-law.

"I understand what you did and why you did it, but I don't know if I could do the same," I said.

"You'll cross that bridge when you come to it," Richard replied. "Once you do, what needs to be done to fix your bad habits and clean up your messes will be very clear. And, it'll be much easier than you think, especially once your team gets on board."

After a quick inspection of our gear, we re-organized ourselves and continued the portage. After about 30 minutes we reached the southwest shore of Range Lake, slipped the canoe into the water and were once again on our way.

"Now that you've seen the error of your ways, it should be smooth sailing for the next two hours," Richard said with a laugh.

Worksheet #5: Life Balance Assessment Survey

Rate yourself based on where you believe you are in life for each of the 16 areas below, using a scale of 1 – 10 (10 being the best). How have you done in each of the following:

1. Finding a fun and exciting business? _____

2. Building a successful relationship with your significant other? _____

3. Building and/or maintaining a close relationship with your family? _____

4. Developing close friendships (not just acquaintances or business contacts)? _____

5. Building your financial resources, strength and flexibility? _____

6. Developing your mental knowledge and strength? _____

7. Maintaining your physical health through diet, exercise and regular exams? _____

8. Developing spiritual depth and peace? _____

9. Increasing your emotional strength? _____

10. Overcoming your fears and living with passion? _____

11. Learning from and teaching wisdom to other people? _____

12. Being of service to others and/or the community? _____

13. Every day self-talk and behavior match your values and mission? _____

14. Managing your time and energy towards your values and mission? _____

15. Rate the quality of the resources you received growing up? _____

16. Rate how you have used those resources as an adult? _____

Total Score (16-160) _____

Worksheet #6: Life Balance Questionnaire

What do you feel you are most proud of accomplishing from the above 16 areas that you could teach to someone else? Who will you teach it to?

1. _____

2. _____

3. _____

Which of the 16 areas do you feel that you will be unable to improve so you need to "accept", "forgive" or "change your perception" so it no longer hurts you? How will you do that?

1. _____

2. _____

3. _____

Which of the 16 areas do you most need to change? What will you do differently?

1. _____

2. _____

3. _____

What three actions will you take in the next two weeks?

1. _____

2. _____

3. _____

Worksheet #6: Life Balance Questionnaire

Who can you delegate actions to or get help from?

1. _____

2. _____

3. _____

Who should you share the result of this questionnaire with?

1. _____

2. _____

3. _____

CHAPTER #6
WORKING TOGETHER WORKS

"Fill their minds with knowledge? Yes. But, most important, give those minds a compass to use the knowledge."
Principal Jacobs (Olympia Dukakis) in Mr. Holland's Opus

The sun was beginning to sink behind the trees, as we made our way to the northern tip of the lake; its warmth immediately diminished as it fell below the tops of the pines.

"We're almost there," Richard said. "Another 20 minutes or so I think."

We had been paddling for over two hours, our progress hampered by a 15 to 20 mile-per-hour head-wind. The wind had brought up a small chop that made paddling more difficult; I had to be careful with each stroke so as not to splash Richard or myself. We had to coordinate our movements carefully in order to be efficient and not lose ground to the wind. When the wind first came up, it took a few minutes to find our rhythm, but we were soon able to dig in and make good time.

When we finally landed on a rocky shore next to a clearing sparsely covered with grass, I was sweaty, tired and very happy to stop paddling. It was obvious someone had camped there recently; a torn plastic grocery bag and an empty beer can were half buried by damp ashes in the fire pit. Several half-burned pieces of fire wood where strewn about.

We knew it would be dark soon, so Richard and I quickly went to work setting up our camp. We untied the gear then dragged the canoe onto the shore and turned it over. Working quickly and quietly, we soon had our tents pitched and a fire started.

"Well, let's see if we can't catch ourselves a little supper," Richard said. He unpacked a telescopic fishing rod, and rummaged through a small tackle box before choosing a silver and orange lure.

"Irresistible," he muttered as he tied it to the line.

He stood up and took a step towards the shore before stopping. "Hey, do you want to do this? If you do, I can get the potatoes boiling."

"No thanks Zen Man, you're the team leader... I just work here."

I filled a pot with lake water and put it on the small grill to boil. I dug through one of the tubs and found a small bag of potatoes. I washed two of them, leaving the skins on, cut them into quarters and plopped them in the water. I added some salt, and then sat with my back to a log and watched Richard through the little bit of smoke our fire was making.

"Aha! Gotcha!" Richard's triumphant shout startled me out of the catnap I had slipped into. I jumped up and ran down to the shore just as Richard reeled a nice-sized fish onto the rocks.

"What's that," I asked.

"It's a smallmouth bass and if you're nice to me,

I'll let you have a bite or two," Richard said grinning from ear to ear.

As he cleaned the fish, I put a frying pan over the flames. When it was hot, I added a little butter and sliced in an onion. Richard filleted the fish onto a plastic plate and we waited for the onions to cook. Once they were done, I put them in a bowl, scraped the pan, added more butter and put in the fillets. I added salt and pepper, and in minutes we were eating.

"This is the second time today I've felt like food never tasted so good," I said.

"Yep, me too," Richard said. "You know, since the slip on the path, we've really come together as a team. This afternoon's paddle was hard work, but we synced up right away and did a great job. And, between your domestic talents and my fearless conquering of wild beasts, we've got our creature comforts under control. Roughing it has never tasted so good."

As I finished my dinner, I began thinking about the day and the conversation we were in the middle of.

"Richard," I said. "We make a pretty good team out here where everything is relatively simple. I'm not so sure I know how to get my team into shape when I go back to the real world... you know, the other real world."

"Well, it all starts with finding the right people," he replied. "I know that sounds simplistic, but it is something many entrepreneurs and business owners do not do on purpose. They tend to hire whoever shows an interest, whoever is handy, relatives, and most often, people like themselves."

"OK, so what do you mean by 'on purpose'?" I asked.

"It starts with a detailed job description for each position. This is something that evolves as you grow and gain experience, but if you do it from the start, you benefit right away."

"That seems straight forward," I said. "But, what do you do to make sure the people you hire fit the bill?"

"The Coach told me that most companies hire based on a resume and perhaps a reference or two. But, that's not enough he says. You also need to have potential employees demonstrate their abilities by asking them to take on a job-specific task, or at the very least, by asking them how they would handle the various challenges they can expect to face."

"But, you said they also had to share your vision."

"That's the other essential element," Richard replied. "A potential employee will need time to fully understand and embrace the company's vision. So, to begin, you need to explore what their most important personal goals are. Also, you need to get to the heart of what makes them tick: their values, their principles, and their personal sense of integrity."

"Whoa, that's heavy. How can you do that in a job interview?"

"The Coach has a method he's shown me that works well. It is really just a series of questions that help the applicant get started in the conversation.

Most people do not consciously define themselves so intentionally, and these questions help them begin examining who they are, why they do what they do, and what they most want out of life."

"It sounds like therapy," I said.

"In a way it is. It is therapy for you too, because it helps you learn to read between the lines and hear what's actually going on beneath the 'interview' personality people present."

"OK, I get it, I think. But, once you hire someone, how do you get them to become part of the team?"

"Communication, communication, communication," Richard said, nodding his head with each repetition of the word. "You have to set up a communication structure that consistently reinforces the company's biggest goals and helps each team member see exactly where they fit in."

"You also have to be constantly listening to what everyone around you is saying, and more importantly, not saying."

"What do you mean?"

"Well, communication has to be two-way and when you are in a position of authority, you need to be aware of how that affects your employees. They often color what they say based on what they think you want to hear, or what they think should be happening. Again, it takes time, but as you practice open, honest communication with your team, you will find they become more trusting, more likely to ask the right questions, and in many ways, much more independent in their ability to think through situations, address problems and take action on their own."

"Man, maybe I'm just tired, but that sounds like a lot of work," I said.

"OK, if you say so," Richard said. I looked at him as I put another small log onto the fire.

"Fine, be that way," Richard said. "But tell me one thing: How much work is it to go through each day not knowing for sure if things are getting done the best way possible? How much work is it to have to go back and clean up mess after mess? How much work is it to have to constantly juggle your family with your business?"

"That's three things," I muttered.

"There's more if you want it," Richard said. "How much of your work is completely wasted? What about all the time you waste? How long have you been limiting your potential and your ability to make a real positive difference in the world?" He stood up, stepped towards me and went on. "What hasn't been done that could have made a difference? What is it too late for already? How has your lack of leadership, courage, honesty, and humility crippled the success of your team? And here's the kicker, how has it hurt your family?"

I just stared up at him. I didn't know how to respond. Part of me felt like jumping up to take a swing at him. Another part wanted to run and hide. But, most of all, I felt deeply saddened.

Richard must have seen all of these emotions play

across my face because he held his hands out, palms facing me, and said, "Whoa there, take it easy. Sorry, I guess I'd better take it easy too. It's been a long day so let's just call it a night and, if you want to, we can talk about this some more in the morning."

I took the pot I cooked the potatoes in, went down to the water, filled it and doused the fire. I rinsed my face, brushed my teeth and crawled into my tent. Even though I was upset, I was also dog-tired and fell fast asleep seconds after my head hit the pillow.

Worksheet #7: Team Assessment

Much of the time, teams have the skills and experience they need and yet their results are mediocre or they lack the energy to sustain great results. Think about yourself as a leader. Think about your top group of leaders or managers – your core team. Think about your company's culture and how it shows up for employees, sub-contractors, suppliers, etc. Rate each of these from 1 – 10.

As a Leader, rate yourself from 1 – 10 (10 as great). Do you:

Interest others in your mission: _____
Involve others' in building your firm: _____
Engage others best strengths: _____
Convince others to commit to results: _____
Inspire others to achieve for the team: _____
Predict performance results accurately: _____
Delegate tasks others can and need to do: _____
Lead the people and manage the processes: _____
Do it, delegate it, or discard it: _____

Total Leader Score:

As a Team, rate your management team from 1 – 10 (10 as great). Does each of you:

Respect each other: _____
Have ambition to achieve: _____
Have the courage to risk: _____
Have strength to persevere: _____
Show wisdom to care for all relationships: _____
Demonstrate trust with each other: _____
Demonstrate competence at getting results: _____
Show discipline in following guidelines: _____
Stay in alignment with each other: _____

Total Team Score: _____

Worksheet #7: Team Assessment

As a Corporate Culture, rate your employees from 1 – 10 (10 as great). Do all of you:

Promote self awareness: _____

Build increasing self esteem: _____

Increase communication and trust: _____

Set and achieve goals together: _____

Teach self control: _____

Become your best selves: _____

Act socially responsible and impacting: _____

Recruit, retain and retire great people: _____

Share stories and myths: _____

Total Culture Score: _____

What do you most need to do to improve your Leadership Abilities?

_____

_____

What do you most need to do to improve your Team?

_____

_____

What do you most need to do to build your Corporate Culture more effectively?

_____

_____

Would this change your Company Vision, Strategies or Team Members? How?

_____

_____

Worksheet #7: Team Assessment

What 3 habits help you to be the best that you can be?

1._____

2._____

3._____

Tough Team Questions

Would I, without a second thought, rehire everyone on my team if I were starting over? Who would I rehire? Why?

Do I sincerely trust everyone on my team? Who do I not trust? Why?

Is everyone on my team a tried and true believer in my/our core values?

If I had to get rid of 2 people, who would they be? Why?

Worksheet #7: Team Assessment

Could I have avoided the above problems with a different hiring or training process? How?

If I was entering my people in a competition, would they be the best trained that they could possibly be? In what areas do I feel that we are the most knowledge and experience deficient?

If I had bad cash flow and knew it would continue for at least 6 months, how long would my people stay with me if I could not afford to pay them? What would I say to them?

If I wanted to hire the best employee for an open position that was critical to me, who are my top 20 A level contacts that I would call?

What proof do I have that our team focuses on the relationship with our customer, not the product?

Worksheet #7: Team Assessment

Your "truck book" helps a back up person take over for someone on your team who was hit by a truck.

Do you have a backup for each position along with an up to date "truck book"? The "truck book" describes what happens if someone on your team was hit by a truck.

What 3 actions will you take in the next 30 days?:

1._____

2._____

3._____

CHAPTER #7
CRISIS IN CAMP

*"Champions take chances and pressure is
a privilege."*
Billie Jean King

I wandered between consciousness and sleep, aware of the tent walls flapping in the wind, but still caught in a dream in which I was standing on a very high hill watching my kids playing with our dog in the backyard. As I watched, my wife opened the patio doors and, as she began speak, I was standing next to her. I knew she didn't know I was there, but in the inexplicable nature of dreams, I also knew if I reached out and touched her, she would turn to me and smile.

As I imagined her smile, there was a great gust of wind outside of my tent. I resisted waking up. I wanted to see my wife smile but an animal grunted and instead of touching my wife, I turned to look towards our backyard. Was it our dog? Another grunt, this one louder and much closer, tore me away from my dream. My eyes shot open only to be greeted by near perfect darkness. I realized there was very little wind and yet my tent was shaking violently. I was frozen with panic but even if I could move, I didn't have a clue about what to do next. I wanted to start screaming like crazy but then thought I might be better off playing dead.

I didn't get a chance to do either as my tent was

suddenly pulled down around me. Tucking my head inside the sleeping bag, I rolled away from the direction the grunts were coming from. Something clamped on to my leg and it took a split second before I realized something was biting me. I tried to kick it with my free foot but was too tightly wrapped in the sleeping bag and the fallen tent. I twisted with all my strength and wrenched my leg free.

I rolled over twice while trying to free myself from the sleeping bag and what was left of my tent. I managed to free my head and arms and during the next roll I saw the stars above me. I rolled again and instead of stars, this time I saw a bear looming over me, illuminated in stark and terrifying detail. If you want to know what my scream sounded like, just imagine the loudest blood curdling scream in the worst "B" horror movie you ever heard and then triple its volume.

I rolled again but came to a sudden stop as my back hit a large pine tree. I was still mummified from the chest down but I could see a flashlight waving madly a few yards away.

"Yah bear!" Richard yelled from behind the beam of light. He ran towards the bear screaming, "Michael, Michael, are you OK?"

I was too stunned to answer. Not only was I in shock from wrestling with the bear, I couldn't believe what I was seeing.

Richard had a flashlight in one hand, and a large tree branch in the other. He was waving the branch and yelling like a crazed warrior in boxer shorts. I actually laughed out loud as I thought, "He's no Mel Gibson, but he certainly has a brave heart."

Richard swung the branch over his head and hit the bear squarely on its rump. He now had the bear's attention and I had a chance to squirm free. I remembered what Moose the outfitter had told me as we loaded the canoes. "If you have any trouble with a bear, stay together, yell and scream. Throw things if you have to and never turn your back and run. Back away but never run."

I groped around on my hands and knees trying to find something to use as a weapon. I clawed a fist-sized rock loose from the dirt and began moving closer to Richard. The flashlight shining in its eyes and Richard's yelling seemed to confuse the bear. I stepped on a branch that snapped loudly. The noise caught the bear's attention and as it swung its head around I threw the best fastball of my life. The rock caught the bear on the side of its head and it bolted into the forest, crashing through the underbrush in a noisy retreat.

Richard was first to relax; he dropped the tree branch, and played the flashlight up and down my body. I still wasn't right in the head because my only thought was, "I'm sure glad I've got my clothes on."

"Are you OK?" Richard asked as he walked towards me. "What are you smiling about?"

"Take a look at you," I said laughing out loud, no longer able to control myself as he turned the light on his legs.

"Are you sure you're OK?" Richard asked again. "Did you hit your head or something, because for a guy who was just about to become bear food, you sure seem happy?"

"No, yeah... I'm OK." I continued to laugh as I reached down to feel my calf. "The tent and sleeping bag saved me."

"Phew that was something else!" Richard exclaimed as he swung the light over to survey what was left of my tent.

The sky to the east was beginning to lighten as we gathered up my gear. The tent was damaged but mostly intact: it was ripped where I had made my escape, there were several small tears from the bear's teeth and two of its peg loops where missing. My sleeping bag wasn't torn at all, but I had burst the zipper getting free of it.

I looked at Richard and said, "Hey, you know we worked well together back there. I guess bears had better think twice before they mess with us."

"Well, I don't know," he replied. "I read somewhere that there are more than 30,000 black bears in Minnesota. Are you ready to take them all on?"

I ignored his joke and said, "Looks like we'll be getting off to an early start today."

"I don't know if we should rush off," Richard said as he examined my tent. "I think we should take it easy. Besides, I would like to fix this tent just in case the weather turns and we need it."

"Oh, let's just go, we can fix that tent tonight," I said.

"Hold on a minute, let's at least have a cup of coffee and a little something to eat."

I knew Richard was right. I was still pumped up on adrenalin and needed to calm down. I gathered up some kindling and built a small fire. Richard got dressed, and prepared his gear for the canoe before picking up my tent. He brought it near the fire, and sat on a log while he worked on it.

"You know Richard, I never pictured bear wrestling as part of our trip. But now that it is over, I think we've got one heck of a story to tell when we get back."

"You're right," he said. "But I can't help but think about what we would be doing right now if you, or me for that matter, had been seriously injured."

His tired and worried expression reminded me about how poorly our previous evening had ended.

"Hey look, about last night… I'm OK with what you said and our fight with the bear shows me we never know when disaster will strike. I can see I've been living and working as if I had all the time in the world. I'm great at jumping into the battle, but not so good at organizing my business, or even my life, in a way that eliminates battles altogether."

Richard only smiled and kept working diligently on the tent.

"You know, the more I think about it, the more I see that I enjoy the rush of dealing with problems. It's like I need to prove how good I am and the only way I can do so is by working all night, or concocting some wild solution to a problem that should never have occurred."

AUTHOR'S NOTE

Teams can meet all sorts of unexpected challenges and overcome even the greatest adversity. Loyalty is a priceless commodity that inspires people to go above and beyond expectations. But it is also important to remember that any team, when faced with an emergency, is capable of heroic acts. The real business heroes are those who remember to hang the food in the tree so there is never an issue with bears. Wading into battle to save the day is one thing, but a great team understands what needs to be done, and then gets it done. A great team prevents the battle from ever happening.

> CHAPTER **WORKSHEETS**

Worksheet #8: The Job Description Process

One of the most effective ways to avoid a state of constant crisis is to start with a solid foundation of capable people. Use the following exercise to define every position in your company.

Step #1: Identification of Deliverables and Competencies
  A. You, or the person in the position, list all of the activities or tasks that must be accomplished.
  B. List all the skills, training and habits required to do a great job.
  C. List all the attitudes required to do a great job.

Step #2: Separate your list into five to seven Key Deliverables (Why do you really pay them?) and Core Competencies.

Step #3: Apply SMART thinking to the Key Deliverables (Specific, Measurable, Agreed To, Reasonable, Time Frame)

Step #4: Build the Scorecard.

Job Title:_____ Example of person in position:_____

Key Deliverables (5-7)

_____
_____
_____
_____
_____
_____
_____
_____
_____
_____

Worksheet #8: The Job Description Process

Core Competencies

Attitude

_____

_____

_____

_____

_____

_____

Skills, Training, Experiences

_____

_____

_____

_____

_____

_____

Definitions

Key Deliverables: Specific, measurable, attainable, reasonable objectives that have a time frame attached to them. Typically desire 4-7 per position. The Key Deliverables can be used to:
   a. measure a fit for a position for a new hire,
   b. evaluate a person already in a position for further development,
   c. determine compensation and bonuses for performance,
   d. run a weekly meeting to determine tactical actions to be taken.

Core Competencies: these are attitudes, skills, training, instincts that we desire to have in a position. While they are important, they may be less measurable than Key Deliverables. Core Competencies are also more typically what is necessary to even be "in the game".

Worksheet #8: The Job Description Process

Examples of Attitude:
Team player
Cheerful
Consistent positive attitude
Willingness to do what it takes

Examples of Skills, Training, Experiences, Habits:
BS in Business Administration
5 years running a team of at least 10 people

Examples of Habits
Contacts the customer every day by 6PM
Has weekly project meeting with three key actions delegated.

Sample: Project Manager Key Deliverables and Core Competencies

Key Deliverables (Ways in which you will be evaluated and rewarded. The bottom line results that we must have):

A. Profitability exceeds bid profit: constantly find ways to increase profit.
"A" player by 2% or more
"B" player by 1-1.9%
"C" player by less than 1%

B. Risk management:
1. All contracts sent out, signed and returned by start of project
"A" players on 100%
"B" players on 85 – 99%
"C" players on less than 84%
2. Identify what was not in the estimate
"A" players within 30 days of the job start in writing to Operations
Manager.
"B" players have completed within 31 – 45 days of the job start.
"C" players complete 45+ days

Worksheet #8: The Job Description Process

C. Close out of job is done in a timely manner with the superintendent and the administrative assistant.
1. Every week all logs and documentation are kept up to date so that within 6 weeks of the job completion, 80% of this work should already be done. This includes all change orders being signed, closing documents are ready for the owner, as built drawings are completed and delivered, punch lists and the operation and maintenance manuals are delivered.
2. Closeout documents submitted to the owner
   "A" players within 15 days of completion of the project
   "B" players within 16 – 30 days of completion
   "C" players 31+ days
3. All monies collected within 30 days of completion.
   "A" players within 30 days
   "B" players will be 31 and 45 days.
   "C" players 46+ days

D. Continuous Improvement: Quarterly choose an action to develop themselves or share their wisdom with the team.
   "A" players do it.
   "C" players do not do it.

Core Competencies (items we need a PM to be good or great at that are needed to support the above Key Deliverables):

1. Attitude:

   a. Team Player
   b. Strong Work Ethic
   c. Positive Attitude
   d. Willing to Learn
   e. Good Listener
   f. Continually improving personally
   g. Assertive
   h. Clear communicator

Worksheet #8: The Job Description Process

2. Skills/Experience:

a. Preferred 4 year degree in an accredited construction-related curriculum (BSCE, BSCM, BSAE, etc.) or equivalent experience to a 4 year degree.

b. Assistant Project Manager experience of 2-3 years, or at least 5 years construction related experience.

c. Demonstrated competency in: estimating, scheduling, budgeting/cost control, field supervision, financial reporting, client relationship, interpersonal skills, computer skills, safety/insurance, communication – written and oral.

d. Generally understand the essential job functions, duties and responsibilities of a Superintendent.

e. Demonstrated proficiency with PC based scheduling and spreadsheet applications, including Microsoft Project, Timberline, Excel and Word.

f. Understand drawings and contract with owners and subs.

g. Negotiate, prepare, issue and execute change orders (proposals) to owners, design team, subcontractors and others. Prepare revisions to original budget as a result of changes and revisions to work.

h. Ensure timely project completion through project scheduling, expediting of materials deliveries and the management of material and document submittals/approvals.

i. Ability to negotiate.

3. Habits:

Daily:
A. Follow-up with architects and owners by 6pm

Weekly:
A. Review cost reports and identify cost risks.
B. Project meetings with subs (take owner and sub logs to meetings and keep updated throughout the week).
C. Keep up Owner Logs and disseminate:

Worksheet #8: The Job Description Process

1) Change Orders with owners
2) RFI with architects
3) Proposal Logs
4) Submittal Logs
D. Keep up Sub Logs and disseminate:
1) Contracts
2) Change orders and proposals
3) RFIs
4) Drawings Log
E. On site at least 2 times per week.
F. Walk site for safety and drawing consistency when on site.
G. 50% in field and 50% in the office.
H. Track change orders and contracts.
I. Update project schedule and disseminate to all parties.

Monthly:
   A. Review cost reports with Joe and John. Prepare for these meetings ahead of time and make sure all attendees get information at least 3 days before the meeting.
   B. Owners meetings
   C. Invoice management: finalize by the 22nd of the month by 9am.

D. Prepare and issue owner progress reports, monthly pay applications, schedules and cost reports in coordination with the Superintendent.

Other:
   A. Insurance certificates on file before subs start the job.
   B. Pre-construction meetings with superintendents and subs.
   C. 100% buyout within 30 days.
   D. Closeout – finalize accounting summaries.
   E. Track change orders and contracts.
   F. 100% buyout within 30 days.
   G. Develop partnership with superintendent.
   H. Provide subs and materials for superintendent in a timely basis.

Contractors Inc. Project Manager Scorecard

Project Manager: _____

Date: _____

Evaluator:_____

Rate the Project Manager from 1-10 on the Scorecard below.

Profitability never exceeds bid profit		Profitability consistently exceeds bid profit by 2%
Contracts are not sent out, signed or returned by the start of the project		All contracts sent out, signed and returned by the start of the project 100% of the time
Does not identify what was not in the estimate within 30 days of the job start or notify in writing the Operations Manager		Identifies what was not in the estimate within 30 days of the job start in writing to the Operations Manager
Logs and documentation are never kept up to date		All logs and documentation are kept up to date weekly including signed change orders
Closeout documents are not submitted to the owner within 15 days of project completion		All closeout documents are submitted to the owner within 15 days of project completion
Monies are consistently collected later than 30 days after project completion		All monies are collected within 30 days of job completion
No goals are established or the goals are not met		Quarterly goals are established and met for skill development
ADD COLUMN TOTALS		TOTALS:___ of ___, Eligible for ___% of bonus pool allocation.

Best At: _____

Most Needs To Improve: _____

Can Teach Others: _____

Top 3 Actions:_____

CHAPTER #8
THE JOURNEY RENEWED

"When planning for a year, plant corn. When planning for a decade, plant trees. When planning for life, train and educate people."
Chinese Proverb

When the coffee came to a boil, I put the pot on a flat stone near the fire. I then found the frying pan, put it over the coals and added six slices of bacon. I poured a cup of coffee and handed it to Richard.

"Thanks," he said. "It's funny about that bear. We hung our food in a tree just like you're supposed to but it still came nosing around. It just shows you can never be too prepared."

The bacon was sizzling, its aroma a sharp contrast to the smoky air. I was calm but I also realized I was starving as if I hadn't eaten for days.

"Man, that bacon smells good," I said reaching for the package. "I think we better cook a little more."

"Hey, we planned for five days, you better take it easy or we'll run out of food," Richard said. "Besides, I think you're just reacting to all the excitement. Why don't we eat what you're cooking now and see what happens?"

I knew he was right, but I also knew we had lots of pancake mix. I prepared the batter and, after the bacon was done, I poured some of the grease out of the pan and used the rest to cook a stack of pancakes.

When everything was ready, I made sure to give Richard an extra pancake.

We ate in silence and it only took a few minutes for us to finish. I cleaned up the dishes, packed them away and put everything in the canoe.

The sun was just coming over the horizon when Richard finished fixing my tent.

"There, it's not as good as new but it will do if the weather changes."

"I think we don't have to worry about that, at least not today," I said. The sky was deep blue without a cloud to be seen in any direction. "I think we're in for an awesome day."

We made our final preparations, slipped the canoe into the water, and paddled out onto the lake. It felt good to be focused on the simple, yet somehow elegant act of paddling. In a few minutes we rounded a bend and the small bay we had camped in opened into a broad lake that looked to be about a half mile wide and very long.

Our plan was to paddle to the end of the lake and then complete a mile-long portage to reach Knife Lake near the Canadian border. We planned to camp on its northern shore and then begin heading back towards Ely.

The day held to its promise of fine weather with only a gentle breeze rippling the waters as we glided along. It took us almost three hours to reach the far end of the lake. We pulled the canoe onto the shore, and shouldering our packs, set off on the portage.

Our progress was slow because the trail was over-grown and very steep in many places. We were ex-hausted by the time we reached the next lake.

"I don't know about you, but I need to take a break," Richard said as he dropped his pack and sat down heavily. He lay back on the pebbly beach, stretched his arms and put his hands behind his head.

"Wow, what an amazing day," he said. "A guy could almost forget about our nasty breakfast guest."

I dropped my pack next to the canoe. I took a step towards the shore, picked up a round, flat stone and skipped it across the glass-like surface of the lake. With each bounce, the rock created a set of circular ripples. Each set grew in circumference until it inter-sected with the next set. The silent collision of ripple to ripple created a lattice work that slowly disap-peared as the serene water absorbed the stone's en-ergy. I contemplated how each bounce had created a unique entity that, as it grew, was immediately altered by its neighbors.

My thoughts turned to the conversation with Rich-ard. I realized we were still right in the middle of it and I wanted to continue even while I resented having to do any thinking whatsoever. I thought how great it would be to just shift my mind into neutral and go on skipping stones for a while. But, seeing the pattern the ripples made gave me a sense there was something significant available to me if I pursued the conversa-tion further.

"Hey, Zen Man, don't go to sleep on me. What about

our plan? Don't we need to stick to our schedule?"

"Oh, we can take it easy for a bit, according to the map, this lake is only six miles long. As long as the wind doesn't come up, we can reach our campsite in three hours."

"OK, but let me ask you something: even if I were crystal clear about my vision and goals for my business, how can I find the perfect team to help me?"

"Ha, now you're asking me the questions," Richard said as he smiled broadly. "Well Grasshopper, it just might be you already have the team you need. What I think you need is a better plan."

He rolled over onto his elbow and looked at me. "The Coach has been using a very interesting analogy in our work together. He says imagine that your company is a baseball team and your vision is to win the World Series."

"Well, I only threw one pitch this morning, but it was a strike," I bragged.

"OK, OK, let's think about it. If your vision for the future is your company's equivalent of the World Series, what do you need to do to win?"

"I guess I need to communicate my vision to the team."

"That's just the beginning," Richard sat up, warming to the conversation. "You need to be sure each player knows their position and is capable of doing their job. That means you must measure performance, and if you want to measure performance, you need to have benchmarks. And, benchmarks are all part of an effective plan. Remember the 'M' in SMART, well having goals that are measurable means your team must also have performance measurements."

"In baseball, everything is under a microscope: hits, runs, errors, strikes, balls... it's all counted and recorded. Do you have something, anything like that for each of your team members?"

I didn't answer right away and Richard went on.

"Business is like baseball. Each year is like a season and each season your goal is to win the World Series. In baseball, the league standings tell you where you are, how many games ahead or behind you are. In business your annual goals give you a way to measure your progress. You can measure how you are doing against your competition, or how well you are able to acquire new capabilities, or how well you maximize your resources."

"In baseball, you keep score in every game. In business, you can create a company scorecard to measure each week as if it were a baseball game. Weekly team meetings enable you to set weekly metrics, acknowledge your tactical successes, and review mistakes and lessons learned."

"Just like in baseball, this method of planning and implementation enables you to make minor adjustments on a week-by-week basis. It also very quickly shows you when major changes are required."

"OK, I get it, but what about the team," I asked. "I don't think I have any Babe Ruths on my team. How do I get them to perform?"

"Well, just like baseball tracks each player's performance, in business you can create individual employee scorecards using a good job description matched with six key deliverables each employee is accountable for."

"But what if they aren't talented or good enough?"

"That's where management has to step in. Part of every employee's scorecard should be a measurement for development. If you are spending time, money and effort on an employee – especially when you find one that is trustworthy and willing to share in achieving your vision – it is wise to invest in their development."

"So, we're back to my vision," I said. "We can't seem to get away from it; my team isn't going to be any good at all if I can't communicate my vision for the business."

"It goes further than that…"

I interrupted Richard saying, "Wait, let me say it: we won't be successful unless each member of my team understands and is motivated by the purpose behind my vision."

"That's right," Richard said smiling broadly and nodding in approval.

"And wait, there's more," I said. "This baseball analogy has me thinking. In baseball, each player is motivated to improve their personal performance because that makes for a longer career and higher salaries. Every pro knows their personal stats and has a plan and training regimen for improvement. Not only is this in the player's best interest, it also works in the best interest of the team."

"You're absolutely right, but there is still more," Richard said, pausing to let me think about what to add.

"I get it," I said. "Management has to put together the team... after figuring out which roles need filling... I guess."

"Right," Richard jumped in. "Not only do you need to determine the roles, you need to acknowledge that we all have different ways of reacting to challenges and different ways of managing responsibility. So, you need to build a structure around your team – made up of systems and capabilities – that acknowledges individual needs while giving each of them what they need to make the greatest possible contribution to the company."

"And it all starts with a common vision and shared goals," I sang out.

"Funny how that works, isn't it?" Richard asked as he looked up at me. "And, let me throw something else at you that the bear reminded me of."

"What now?" I interrupted him again. "Are you going to tell me bears are like baseball?"

He laughed. "No, seriously, think about it, if you are not clear about your purpose and the vision it creates for your business, where is the excitement?"

"What do you mean?"

"Would you play a game, any game, without keeping score? If you're just putting in time, and have no way of measuring progress, no goals to celebrate, you can fall into the practice of management by crisis. Because there is no passion for doing things based on clear goals and measurable results, you find the only excitement you get is when you're putting out fires. So, over time – and most business owners don't even see this – you actually start fires just for the thrill of putting them out."

"Um, the bear, what about the bear?" I asked as I picked up another perfectly flat, round and smooth stone.

"Oh yeah, scaring off the bear was a real crisis and I must say, it was a thrill handling that crisis, especially since it ended well for us. But, in business, one of the first things you need to do in order to stop managing by crisis is to distinguish between a real crisis, something important that requires your immediate attention, and lesser problems, events, or interruptions that do not qualify as a true crisis."

"Hold it," I said skipping the stone and then turning towards Richard. "Do you mean to tell me you think I always manage by crisis? That's pretty sneaky, using the bear to get at me like that. You're good!"

"Well, maybe not all of the time, but you said so yourself that very few days go by without some sort of problem showing up."

"OK, you got me, go on."

"Well, the next step is to see that when crisis management is the norm rather than the exception, it usually means there are more fundamental problems to be solved."

"Not the vision thing again," I moaned.

"Well, it could be that, but the Coach uses an old Chinese proverb that says the superior doctor prevents sickness, while the mediocre doctor attends to impending sickness, and the inferior doctor treats sickness. To figure out what needs to be fixed next time there is a crisis, don't just treat the symptoms, cure the underlying disease and prevent it from recurring."

"Man, I'm exhausted just thinking about all of this. Hadn't we better get back on the water," I said, picking up my paddle and pushing the canoe off the rocky shore.

"Wait a second," Richard said handing me an energy bar. "You better eat something or we'll be having another crisis."

AUTHOR'S NOTE

On using Scorecards

When doing evaluations for any element of your life or business, or developing a team brainstorming session, or aligning the most important actions of your most important relationships, there are five key obstacles:

1. Spending time can "feel" like a lot of effort to do so we never begin.
2. We are not sure where to go next after the initial, obvious perceptions.
3. We do not create a baseline that provides context and a sense of progress for future evaluations and brainstorming.
4. We are trying to evaluate gut feelings and instincts about issues that are hard to qualify (and quantify).
5. The reactions of our team to the topic may be negative.

With our clients, and ourselves, we very successfully use scorecards to identify the 8 to 15 critical elements of any issue. We define a 10 as a home run and a 1 as a strike out.

This allows us to:
1. Reduce the amount of time spent discussing "fuzzy" stuff with little action.
2. More easily evaluate an area of life or business together.
3. Clarify and test that we are truly identifying the critical elements.
4. Crystallize thinking and feeling as objectively as possible.
5. Facilitate a creative brainstorming session where we compare evaluations and share perceptions.

6. Identify "next steps to take" with clear accountability.
7. Use our baseline "total score" to motivate and measure ongoing progress.

Bottom line: This will help your team to clearly align their perceptions and actions of an area in their life or your business and best determine the most important priorities for progress towards your vision.

The Sales Scorecard

This is an example of a scorecard that can be used by Sales Managers, a Sales Team or an owner when working to identify and improve sales results.

For your sales department, we would like you to rate your current satisfaction from 1 – 10 with 10 being perfect in every way and 1 being extremely unsatisfactory. Add up column totals to get your score.

Our Sales Process is not in writing and different with each customer		Our Sales Process is in writing with the definition of advances and deliverables and experiences
We do not have a clear snapshot of our salespeople's activity		Weekly reporting by a salesperson regarding advances and continuations are reviewed by the sales manager
The sales manager discusses the sales call afterwards		Pre-call coaching, training and role-playing of salespeople is done by the sales manager
We do not evaluate our salespeople other than on sales achieved		We use written definitions of A, B and C salespeople
We have sales tools that are gathering cobwebs		We have a Sales Toolbox that is built, used and updated at least annually
Our sales team does not care what else happens in the rest of our business		Our sales team buys into our long term vision
Sales and the rest of our team have conflicts		Sales and the rest of our team work very well together
Product/services are not updated until we are pushed by competition		Product/services are being developed and tested regularly with customer feedback
We are not clear on the value each customer brings to us		Customers are evaluated at least annually and rated as an A, B, or C customer
Marketing and sales are not in alignment		Marketing supports sales and sales supports marketing with a free flow of important information
Our salespeople are not performing		We are regularly hiring sales superstars, developing existing salespeople and culling out the deadwood
ADD COLUMN TOTALS		YOUR SCORE

CHAPTER 9
A REFRESHING DISCOVERY

"A great dream with the wrong team is a nightmare.
If your dream is bigger than the team, you have to
give up your dream or grow up your team."
Author Unknown

We had been paddling in silence for about two hours when I noticed smoke rising over the trees about a half-mile ahead of us.

"Looks like we're not the only hardy adventurers up here," I said quietly.

"Yeah, you're right. Why don't we drop in and say hello? Besides I need to eat something and I sure am getting thirsty."

As we drew closer, I could see the smoke was coming from a small island separated from the shore by a narrow channel. The still air left the smoke undisturbed as it rose in a straight, languidly dissipating column. Despite the steepness of the shore, a weathered rowboat had been dragged up to the tree line twenty feet from the water. As I hopped out of the canoe and steadied it for Richard, I saw the boat was sitting atop three birch logs. I realized the logs had been used to roll the boat up to its high mooring.

We pulled the canoe ashore and tied it to one of the rowboat's oarlocks. We scrambled up the embankment using the roots of a large pine tree for hand holds and stairs. When I reached the top, I was surprised by a scene that immediately reminded me of something from Grimm's Fairy Tales. A few feet in front of a small, roughly built cabin, a cauldron was suspended on a metal tripod over a smoldering fire. Tendrils of steam rose from the cauldron and I sniffed the air as I walked forward. I could smell a sweet, herbal aroma that I recognized but couldn't place. Close by, bunches of a leafy plants hung upside down on a rack made from willow branches.

I was almost close enough to look into the cauldron when a woman's voice boomed from behind me, "Hey buddy, what's new?"

She laughed as I spun around. "Sorry son. Didn't mean to scare you. Looks like you've seen a ghost. Am I really that hard on the eyes?" she asked as she walked towards me.

"No, no…" I stammered as I backed away from her.

"Watch out or you'll find yourself in the fire if you're not careful." She smiled, crow's feet deepening around her eyes. Her white hair was tied in a single ponytail that went halfway down her back. Her clear grey eyes sparkled with mischief as they held mine.

Richard came to my rescue. "Hello. You must be Helen." He stepped forward with his hand out and said, "My name is Richard and my nervous friend here is Michael. He had a rough morning so you'll have to forgive him."

As they shook hands I just stood there, mouth open and thought "What the heck is happening here?"

They both laughed as they turned to look at me. "Cat got your tongue?" the woman asked.

"No, more like a bear," Richard said. He was grinning from ear-to-ear.

"You two know each other…" I said, my voice trailing off with doubt.

"No, no never met the man before," Helen said. "But if you have the time, I'm sure we can get acquainted. Come, sit down and I'll get you a drink."

I looked at Richard with astonishment as he stepped towards a table made from planks cut with a chain saw. He shrugged off his pack and sat down. I didn't move. "Hey, relax. Helen is famous. When I read about her, I asked Moose to set up our trip so we could use her place as a turning point. From here on in we head back to civilization."

"You're famous?" I asked Helen as she came back from behind the cabin. She was carrying two old-fashioned, swing-top bottles. They were dripping wet and when she handed one to me, I realized they were very cold.

"There's a little spring-fed creek out back that keeps these beauties nice and chilly. I always have some on hand because you never know who will drop in."

"Helen is famous," Richard repeated. "Take a drink if you want to find out why."

I pushed the metal bails with my thumbs and the ceramic lid opened with a loud pop. I sniffed at the top of the bottle, carbon dioxide tickled my nose and once again I smelled that familiar aroma. "Go ahead, it won't hurt you," Helen said grinning and putting her hands on her hips.

I was trying to figure out exactly what Richard was up to as I lifted the bottle to my lips. The cold, effervescent liquid fizzed on my tongue and the carbon dioxide brought tears to my eyes. "It's root beer!" I shouted.

I took a great long drink emptying half the bottle. It tasted like no root beer I ever had before. Instead of being overly sweet, it was clean and crisp and its flavor reminded me of trees and herbs.

"I make it with wintergreen," she said. "There's plenty of it in the forest around here. It's the bush with little white flowers that look like they're nodding their heads. You can eat the berries and chew the leaves if you want the real wintergreen experience."

"You make this here?" I asked.

"Yup, quite a few bottles, more every year. It seems living alone in the wilderness doesn't mean you have to be lonely... not as long as you make root beer."

"See, I told you she was famous." Richard drained the last of his bottle and said, "Hey Helen, can we get a couple more bottles of your best brew?"

As she went back behind the cabin Richard handed me an energy bar and told me she was once a teacher in a large city. He said she had moved out here to run an inn but the government had kicked everyone out when the wilderness area was established. Somehow she had managed to stay and now she lived by herself making and serving bottles of root beer to passing canoeists.

As I drank the second bottle, more slowly this time, I realized just how good it was. Its complex, spicy flavor was hard to pin down: one moment it reminded me of licorice, then bubble gum, and even a hint of vanilla crept in from sip to sip.

"This is amazingly good," I said. "How do you do it?"

Well, I might as well have asked a neurosurgeon to explain the inner workings of the human brain. Helen walked me through the entire process from finding the ingredients to preparing the equipment, mixing a batch, fermentation times, and how long to age it after it had been bottled.

She showed me the binder she used to record the details of each batch. It contained pages and pages about every aspect, every variation and every contingency she had encountered in the root beer making process. She called it her recipe book.

Forty minutes later Richard again came to my rescue.

"Helen, Michael and I have to be going. We need to get to the end of the lake and set up camp before it gets dark."

We offered to pay for the root beer but Helen refused.

"Just meeting you two gentlemen is payment enough," she said. "You could do me a little favor though, let Moose know I need some packets of brewers yeast. He usually sends them up with one of his customers."

We promised we would pass the message on, said our goodbyes, picked up our packs and clambered back down to the canoe.

As I leaned into my paddle and we glided along, I felt as if I had just been touched by something special. At first it seemed so out of place to find an old woman in the middle of the wilderness making root beer. But, as she spoke to me, I saw she was in step with the natural world around her. She had intimate knowledge of her surroundings and was at peace with them. She was able to take what nature provided and use it to create something unexpected, extraordinary, and unforgettable.

After paddling for an hour we came upon a small clearing along the shore. Richard said he thought we had gone far enough so we landed and quickly set up camp.

"Tonight's menu is special," Richard said as he dug through the tub holding our food. "I'm going to make you the best olive oil, garlic, sun-dried tomato pasta you've ever had."

"Wow, what a day. One experience after the other, nothing I expected and it just keeps getting better and better." I watched Richard as he unwrapped a small paring knife and began dicing a clove of garlic. "What can I do to help?" I asked.

"Not much, just fill this pot with water and then have a seat and relax."

As I watched Richard work, I thought about our

ongoing conversation. I wondered how he would use the root beer lady as an object lesson for building a business and life filled with meaning and purpose. I knew he must have something up his sleeve.

"That Helen is quite a character," I said, hoping to prompt him into telling me how she fit into the bigger picture.

"She sure is. Boy, were you ever funny when you first saw her."

That's all he said. I knew he was probably waiting for me to start up the conversation, but I didn't feel like giving him the satisfaction, especially not after all of the laughs he had already enjoyed at my expense.

The dinner was superb. The exercise, excitement of the day, and fresh air combined to make Richard's wilderness gourmet cooking that much better.

"Well, you sure put that meal together," I said as a compliment to Richard's cooking.

"Well, just like Helen, I've been working on the recipe for quite some time."

"Aha!" I exclaimed. "Now you're going to tell me how important it is for me to refine my vision and goals, my team, my processes, and everything else I need in order to have the perfect business."

Richard gave me his best 20,000-megawatt smile and said, "Well grasshopper, it would appear that that is no longer necessary."

"Ah come on," I moaned. "Isn't there more to it? What is this all about?"

Richard leaned forward, his smile disappeared and

he said, "Of all the lessons I've learned over the years, the one I still have the most difficulty accepting and applying is that you never reach a point where everything is perfect. The Coach helped me understand you have to continuously strive to improve everything; you can never stop. And, even though I get it on an intellectual level, from time to time, I feel a little ripped off. Why can't good enough just be good enough?"

Richard looked down at his plate, and stabbed at a piece of pasta. "I have learned that when I'm feeling like I could just settle for what I've already done, that's when it is most important for me to revisit the meaning of my work."

"Well, making root beer is pretty meaningful," I quipped.

"Look, take this seriously. Helen may not appear to be the best example of someone who is building a business and life around meaning. But think about it. Think about the experience you had while visiting her. Because she is where she wants to be, comfortable in her own skin, living in harmony with her surroundings and knows how to make the most of what's available to her, she projects a profound sense of purpose combined with serenity and grace. And, through intention, diligence, patience, constant refinement, and vision she was able to give you two of the most perfect bottles of root beer ever to pass your lips. You'll never taste better. Well, you'll never taste better until the next time you visit her and by then I can guarantee she'll have taken the art of root beer brewing to the next level."

I smiled at Richard as he paused for a breath. A few seconds of silence passed before I said, "Let me give it a try. Helen's root beer is a metaphor for taking things to a deeper level. I get that. But she is just one person. She doesn't have a team to manage, clients to please, a family to care for or – apparently at least – bills to pay."

"That's right, but can you imagine what would happen if she was transplanted into a team situation while being encouraged to continue blossoming as she has been doing on her own?"

"Well," I replied. "That would certainly take some inspired leadership to pull off."

"Ah grasshopper, that's your half-thought of the day," Richard said, smiling to let me know he was kidding me. "Think about what would happen if you had a person like Helen on your team. People like her take responsibility for what they do. They bring desire and curiosity along with tremendous energy and love to their work. They are leaders in and of themselves and God only knows what a team of leaders like Helen could accomplish."

My mind was swimming with thoughts and emotions as I tried to wrestle with everything that had happened and everything Helen and Richard were teaching me. "Let me try to put this all together..."

"Wait a minute, it's dark, we've had an exceptionally tiring day, so I think that's enough for tonight. We've only got two more days and a lot of water to cover before we get back to Ely. Why don't you get some sleep and we'll pick up our conversation in the morning when we're rested and can see things more clearly."

Richard was right, I was suddenly aware that I was tired to my very core. I nodded in agreement, washed up at the lake, changed my clothes and crawled into my damaged tent.

As I tucked the sleeping bag around me to make up for the broken zipper, my mind was racing and I thought I would never get to sleep. At first I worried about another bear attack and then began thinking about everything else that had happened. I realized I had just been through one of the most amazing and meaningful days of my life.

Author's note

The character of Helen is based on a real person named Dorothy Molter. As a child, I visited her while on a canoe trip with my father and I, like many other people, always knew her as the "Root Beer Lady". She lived on the Isle of Pines on Knife Lake for more than 56 years until her death in 1986.

If you are interested in her story, you can visit the Dorothy Molter Museum, which is managed by the Dorothy Molter Memorial Foundation and is located in Ely, Minnesota.

> CHAPTER **WORKSHEETS**

Worksheet #9: The Recruiting, Retaining and Retiring Quiz

This quiz provides key questions you can ask when trying to increase your success in achieving the "3 R's"
• Recruiting great employees
• Retaining the best "A" and "B" employees
• Retiring the "C" employees

What are your 3 best sources that can "refer" great employees to you?

1. _____

2. _____

3. _____

What are the top 5 reasons that you are unable to recruit great employees?

1. _____

2. _____

3. _____

4. _____

5. _____

What is the exact dollar cost of making a mistake in hiring? $_____
How many employees do you have to hire to keep 1 great employee? _____

Do managers and employees willingly participate in Recruiting, Retaining and Retiring great employees? i.e. How many referrals to potential hires have you

Worksheet #9: The Recruiting, Retaining and Retiring Quiz

gotten from existing employees in the last 12 months? _____

For each employee that enters the hiring process, how many employees invest at least 15 minutes with them? _____

In hiring interviews, do you share the position job description and does it have clear measurable goals that define an "A" player? Yes_____ No _____

How do you test to make sure you are hiring an employee with the right instincts?

_____

How do you test to make sure you are hiring an employee with the right skills?

_____

How do you test to make sure you are hiring an employee with the right values?

_____

Is there a written process for interviewing, debriefing and evaluating potential hires as a team? Yes_____ No_____

How do you interview, assess and measure candidates' abilities and past accomplishments at guiding and handling major change?

_____

Do you have a written and consistent orientation and training program that reinforces values, teaches new resources and reinforces company goals and vision? Yes_____ No_____

What are the top 5 reasons that you are unable to retain great employees?

1. _____

2. _____

Worksheet #9: The Recruiting, Retaining and Retiring Quiz

3. _____

4. _____

5. _____

Is weekly reporting of key metrics in place for the company, each department and each position?
Yes_____ Monthly _____ Quarterly _____ Annually_____ No_____

Are the job descriptions clear, simple and directly support company, department and position goals? Yes_____ No _____

What is the process for managing the performance of employees across the organization?

_____

How many hours last month did you invest in coaching, debriefing, evaluating and teaching employees behaviors and the organization's values and goals? _____ hours

How many hours last month did your direct reports invest in coaching, debriefing, evaluating and teaching employees behaviors and the organization's values and goals? _____ hours

Is there a consistent process for rewarding and recognizing employees?
Yes_____ No_____

Is there a consistent process for evaluating promotion candidates against organizational values? Yes_____ No_____

How many employees were fired in the last 12 months? _____ Quit? _____ Are there consistent criteria for firing employees? Yes_____ No_____

Worksheet #9: The Recruiting, Retaining and Retiring Quiz

Does your current org chart accurately reflect any new directions you desire to take?
Yes_____ No _____

How many positions have a written career path? _____ positions. How many do not have a career path? _____ positions.
Why?_____

What is your process for helping your employees to retire? _____
_____

Observations:

1. _____

2. _____

3. _____

4. _____

5. _____

Actions To Take:

1. _____

2. _____

3. _____

4. _____

5. _____

CHAPTER 10
HEADING HOME

"Gabriel pressed his point: 'That is a question, David Ponder. Are your emotions and resolve controlled by circumstances?'
'No, they are not,' David said firmly.
'That is correct,' Gabriel nodded. 'Circumstances do not push or pull. They are daily lessons to be studied and gleaned for new knowledge and wisdom. Knowledge and wisdom that is applied will bring about a brighter tomorrow. A person who is depressed is spending too much time thinking about the way things are now and not enough time thinking about how he wants things to be.'"
Excerpt from "The Traveler's Gift" by Andy Andrews

The ozone smell of approaching rain woke me. I knew the sun had risen but the grey, diffused light told me the morning must be heavily overcast. I crawled from my tent and looked out across the lake. As I scanned the horizon, I could not tell where the water and clouds met as yesterday's sparkling blue water had been replaced with a dull, metallic-grey mirror.

Richard was trying to coax a flame from kindling piled on the remains of the previous night's fire. "Hey Michael, good morning," he said quietly, his voice muffled by the damp, close air. "It looks like we may be in for some wet weather."

"Yeah, I can smell it coming," I said, hugging myself as a shiver passed through my body. "Look on the bright side, we are going to get a chance to use that rain gear we've been lugging around."

"Well, as long as the wind doesn't come up, we'll be OK. Let's get some coffee in us and then pack up the tents before the rain hits," Richard said, as he poured the grounds from a plastic container into the basket of our soot-blackened, tin percolator.

Despite the grey, damp morning, I felt rested, calm and clear headed. "Richard?"

"Yes Michael."

"Last night I was about to launch into my version of everything we've talked about and the lessons I've learned on this trip…"

"So far," Richard interrupted. "The lessons you've learned so far. This trip isn't over yet."

"Well, that's true but I want to give it a try anyway."

"That's OK by me." Richard smiled as he poured coffee into a cup and handed it to me.

Steam rose from the near boiling liquid. The coffee's aroma was wonderful but I had to wait for it to cool before sipping. I blew on the coffee, stretched my back and neck, took a deep breath and began.

"So, it all starts with me… that's right, it's all about me," I said, somewhat surprised at what I just said. I smiled ruefully and went on, "When I got into your airplane, I was a mess. I was struggling with doubt.

My sense of who I am and what I am about had been taking quite a beating. But, the last few days have helped me see that my definition of self, of what I am all about, is weak to begin with. It lacks definition."

I paused. I was not looking at Richard as I had been staring into the steaming coffee cup I held in my palms. Its warmth was comforting and made it easier for me to open up and speak from the heart. I took a sip and raised my eyes toward Richard. His expression invited me to continue. It seemed as though he needed to hear whatever it was I was going to say.

"This weak definition of who I am has been the cause of almost every single problem. Because I do not have a powerful sense of purpose, my actions, my business and really, my life, all lack meaning."

"It limits the amount of energy and passion I can bring to the challenges I face. Because I am unclear in my own mind, I am unable to lead others. They may not understand why, but they instinctively sense something is missing. They may try to put in stuff of their own, to fill in the gaps, but it doesn't work because it's not exactly what I want. Or, because my passion is lacking, they just don't care, they are not compelled to bring their passion to the table."

"Across the board, I mean with everyone around me, I have not shared my true purpose and my most important goals. How can I expect people to line up with me, to give it all they've got, when I haven't even given them a chance to understand what it's all about? They have no way of knowing if my goals align with theirs."

As I was speaking, Richard put his coffee cup down and walked towards me. He stood directly in front of me and grabbed my shoulders. "Look at you, Mr. Grasshopper, you are really getting it. There's one thing I want you to add. I think it will help," he said, releasing my shoulders.

"What's that'" I asked.

"You must remember that even though everything starts with you, most of the people around you are in the same boat. They haven't done this type of thinking either. They, like you, build their lives by accident. They haven't done the work needed to figure out what their true purpose is and what their most important goals are. If you understand this, you can begin to accept it."

"Accept it! What do you mean? Isn't that giving up?"

"No, no, no," Richard said smiling at me. "I guess I should have said 'acknowledge' instead of 'accept'. Knowing people do not have clear goals gives you an incredible opportunity to show leadership. By becoming crystal clear about your goals, your purpose, you acquire the integrity and the power to help other people discover their own purpose and goals. In fact, if you are trying to build a winning team, you need to demand they do the work and get as clear as possible about their life's meaning."

"Man, oh man, you are something else," I said. I wanted to go on, but I wasn't sure what to say next. To buy some time I said, "Hey, Zen Man, we better pack up and get going while it's still dry."

It took us very little time to strike camp and pack the canoe. We pushed off into the lake and after a few paddle strokes, I asked Richard what he thought the day ahead would be like.

"Oh, I think it will be a day of great personal clarity, mixed with some rain showers and the occasional epiphany."

I laughed and shook my head, "OK, so how much paddling, portaging and pontificating is ahead?"

"We've got to get through this lake, it's another seven miles or so. A half-mile portage will then get us to the second to last lake of our journey. It's about eight miles long. From there, we have a short portage and, if all goes well, we'll be able to get back to our first campsite on Burntside Lake before nightfall. If we are really lucky, the other canoe and your favorite outboard motor will still be there."

"Pontificating, you forgot to give me the pontificating forecast," I teased.

Richard ignored my joke so I went on, "OK, clearly I need to get my act together on the goals and purpose thing. But, I'm not sure I can do it right this second so I want to go forward and try to describe the next steps."

"Michael, I think that's a great idea. You know, you don't need to force yourself into saying something that doesn't ring absolutely true with you. Sometimes ardently pursuing a thing only serves to chase it away. Now that you realize the need for clarity, it will come to you."

Richard stopped for a minute, chuckled to himself and muttered, "I really am starting to sound like 'Zen Man'."

"The next step is to work on my goals," I said, smiling at Richard's self-admonishment. "In business it is imperative to set SMART goals. This makes it easier for everyone on the team to understand the goals and their role in achieving them. It also gives us a structure for measuring progress."

I stopped speaking for a few minutes and listened. Our steady, rhythmic paddling made very little noise. Birds were chirping and trilling in the dense forest on the nearby shore. A slight breeze ruffled the water and rattled leaves.

"SMART is pretty smart," I began again. "Articulating goals that are specific, measurable, agreed to, realistic, and have a time frame has, in and of itself, got to make a big difference for any company and any team. A business plan made up of SMART goals has got to be a winner."

"That's right," Richard chimed in. "You will also notice setting SMART goals actually helps you and your team further clarify your purpose. It's kind of organic in how it works. You become better at communicating with each other which, in turn, leads to increasingly constructive and meaningful conversations and greater clarity."

Neither of us spoke for a long while.

As I tried to put what I was learning to work, I began to experience what Richard had described when he said clarity would come to me. As I was thinking through how to create a business plan utilizing SMART goals, an image of the future formed in my mind. I saw my team working together as smoothly as Richard and I were paddling. A deep sense of purpose ran through every conversation and meeting. Each one of us was doing the things we loved and I was free to plan, create, and innovate. We all spoke from a shared frame of reference. We all understood, respected and supported each other. We were able to accomplish whatever we set our minds to.

"Here we are," Richard said, his words jolting me back to the present. "Let's just pick up the canoe and get this portage over with. We'll have some lunch when we get to the other lake."

We had become very proficient in handling the canoe and our gear. We lifted the canoe over our heads with a well-coordinated heave and set off. I was reminded of how I had dropped the canoe during the first portage.

"So, a plan built on SMART goals also forces you to look at your abilities, your teams' skills, the business systems, business processes and all that stuff," I said, my words echoing inside the canoe.

"It really makes you see the need to improve everything and, based on what I've seen so far, it really compels you to clean up your messes and make repairs to anything that isn't working."

Richard said, "That's right. At first it can be daunting because there is a lot to do. But, over time, you and your team will acquire a habit of continuous improvement. In fact, done properly, your business plan will always include time and resources for working on the business."

A gust of wind rushed through the forest bringing with it the first drops of rain. We trudged on, staying dry under the canoe. When we reached the shore of the next lake, we quickly pulled our rain gear from our packs and slipped it over our clothes.

Richard handed me an apple and two energy bars and I slowly munched my way through them. I took a long, deep drink of water from my canteen, put it back into the webbing on the outside of my pack and stowed the pack in the canoe. We pushed off into the rain-splattered lake, the tiny ripples from each drop co-mingling and reminding me of the ripples formed by the stone I skipped two days before.

"Hey Richard, are we having fun yet?" I yelled as a gust of wind carrying more rain swept across the lake. Its impact deflected the canoe and we had to compensate by paddling harder.

"You bet!" he yelled with delight. I knew he was having a blast. There was nothing like a little challenge to get him going and I could picture him behind me with an ear-to-ear grin.

The wind had come up and although it was slowing our progress, it was also pushing the rain clouds across the sky. In an hour the rain stopped and the clouds began to break up. As the sun reappeared, the wind died down and I began to sweat inside of my rain gear.

"Let's take a break and get this rain gear off," I said. We had been staying close to the shore and with a few strokes we landed on a small beach of white pebbles.

After folding up and packing my rain suit, I said, "Now, let me think about this baseball analogy you described. As I understand it, the baseball analogy helps you develop a management structure to ensure your business plan is implemented successfully."

"That's right," Richard replied. "And, if you can tell me how it works, I might even stop calling you 'grasshopper'."

"OK… it starts with defining your World Series. That means you need to define what a championship looks like for your company. You then look at each year as a season and keep a league score to monitor your wins and losses based on competitive and business goals. You then break that down to keep score on a game-by-game basis – really that's a week-by-week basis. Finally, each player has their own scorecard to track individual performance along with their personal plans for improving skills and addressing weaknesses."

I was smiling broadly at Richard waiting to be congratulated on my answer.

"Ah, grasshopper, you have come far, but there is sill much you need to learn."

"What do you mean?" I demanded.

"Well, you get almost 100% for your description,

but one thing I want you to add is that each team member, from owner down to bat boy, needs a simple, practical description of their job. This includes responsibilities, accountabilities, and the appropriate benchmarks for measuring performance."

"That's it?"

"No, you also need to remember that for this structure to work, you need to meet each week with your team to review the previous week and plan ahead. This enables you to track hits, runs, errors and, as you learn what is working and what needs fixing, adjust your plan as needed."

"I would have gotten there soon enough," I protested despite having forgotten all about job descriptions and the weekly meetings.

We got back into the canoe and set off. After a few minutes Richard spoke up and asked, "Do you want to keep going? I mean keep talking through what you've learned?"

"Sure," I said as I gathered my thoughts. "Once you have the necessary systems and processes in place, you're better able to control how you spend your time, effort and resources. I don't know how you managed to arrange it, but the fight with the bear showed that I have fallen into the habit of managing by crisis. And, that's because I not only lacked clear goals and a plan, I also had no way of measuring progress and knowing what was most important."

"And, speaking of arranging things, the root beer lady was a stroke of genius. Meeting Helen put a very fine point on the necessity to refine and refine again; to constantly take things deeper, to never stop striving for perfection. In fact, it's almost as if the journey to perfection, to an ideal model, is in and of itself one of the most important purposes of a business, of a team… and I guess, an individual. Me."

My words seemed to hang in the air and follow us along as we paddled. I again had the feeling that clarity was coming to me. Just as I was paddling to get to the end of the lake, the thinking and talking about what it meant to be a business owner was taking me to a destination. I did not know what the end of the lake looked like, but I knew I would recognize it when we arrived.

I was done thinking about things at that point. As excited as I was about making real progress, I was also exhausted physically and mentally. When we reached the far shore, I realized Richard was probably in the same shape because we didn't say anything as we hoisted the canoe and carried it across the short portage and dropped it into Burntside Lake.

It took another hour to reach the island where we had left the outboard motor and the other canoe. The sun was beginning to set as we quickly and silently made camp and prepared a simple dinner of beans and campfire toast.

Sitting around the fire, we made small talk about friends and our families. I brought Richard up to date on my kids and he told me about a new business venture he was looking into.

"Well, I think it's time to pack it in," Richard said, standing and stretching. "We covered more ground today than the previous two days combined. We're getting good at this."

"You're not kidding," I said. "I feel like I've made more progress today than at any other time in my life." Richard looked across the fire at me and smiled. "Yes you have... yes you have," he said. He turned away and began washing up.

Even though it was coming to an end, the entire trip seemed to be present all around me. It was with me as I crawled into my tent and lay there thinking. I wanted to package it up, make it into a movie or something so I could replay the whole thing over and over. I realized I was very close to discovering something extremely important but I couldn't find the last few keys, or see the last few stepping-stones I needed in order to complete my journey. The day was over, but I felt as if my life was just about to begin.

> CHAPTER **WORKSHEETS**

Worksheet #10: The Personal PMG Connector

Many people set goals that are way out there but they do not often figure out how to achieve those goals. They are more like wishes than real goals. In order to actually achieve your goals, you need to set out a sequence of stages and steps for getting there. Completing this exercise will help you develop a sequence for achieving your goals and, if you fill in goals in each category, it will help you achieve greater balance in your life and business.

Name:_____   Date:_____

		10 Years	5 Year	3 Year	1 Year
1	Personal:				
2	Health:				
3	Spiritual:				
4	Significant Other:				
5	Family & Friends:				
6	Business/Career:				
7	Core Team:				
8	Travel:				
9	Toys/Hobbies:				
10	Financial:				
11	Community:				

Worksheet #10: The Personal PMG Connector

What I learned doing this was:

1. _____

2. _____

3. _____

I need to share these goals with the following 3 people since they can help support, teach or guide me:

1. _____

2. _____

3. _____

I will accomplish the action plan and stay focused on my goals by:

_____

I will review my worksheet on   /   /   (date)

CHAPTER 11
DESTINATION MEANING

*"I am of the opinion that my life belongs to the
community, and as long as I live, it is my privilege to
do for it whatever I can. I want to be thoroughly used
up when I die, for the harder I work, the more I live.
Life is no 'brief candle" to me. It is a sort of splendid
torch which I have got hold of for a moment, and I
want to make it burn as brightly as possible before
handing it on to future generations."*
George Bernard Shaw

The next morning, a slight breeze, a flawless sky,
bird songs and the smell of frying bacon greeted
me as I emerged from my tent. Richard walked by,
coming from the lake. He was carrying the coffee pot
and it was dripping water on his boots and pant legs.
Smiling, he nodded in my direction. I nodded back
but neither of us spoke while he prepared breakfast
and I packed my gear in preparation for the journey's
last leg.

When I finished packing, I sat on a log with my
back to the fire. As I scanned the surroundings, I began
to feel as though the passage of time was slowing. My
senses became acute. Beyond the smoke and cooking
food, I could smell lake water, the damp forest floor,
the freshness of the leaves in the trees, and the sharp
perfume of pine tar. My vision was clear. I could see
each tree as a separate entity distinct from the forest,

each leaf distinct from the other. I could hear the rattle of small rocks as ripples and small waves lapped at the shore. The rustle of leaves and the shrill cry of a hawk were joined by the sound of my beating heart.

I can't explain why, but I knew that if I uttered even a single word, the spell would be broken and the future would invade this achingly perfect present. But unfortunately, merely thinking of the future was enough, it was not to be denied and my thoughts raced ahead to when our trip would end. The moment was lost and my euphoria was displaced by a tremor of dread at the thought of returning to wage the battle my life had become.

"Hey Michael, what's happening," Richard asked quietly as he poured coffee into a cup.

"Oh, not much, just soaking it all in, trying to enjoy the moment," I said, swinging my feet over the log and reaching for the cup Richard was offering.

"I don't think I've ever seen a morning more perfect than this," he said. "Well, all good things must come to an end. Let's eat this grub and then take a stab at putting those two canoes together."

"This morning is beyond perfect, I wish every day, no every moment, could be like this," I said. "I can't remember ever feeling so relaxed, so at peace as I do right now, right here."

"I know what you mean. Things are very simple here. There are only a very few things that really need to get done. Our bodies and minds are taking comfort from nature and the simplicity of merely paddling and taking care of our own, personal basic human needs. We are tapping into a much more natural way of life, one that works with nature not against it."

"Wow, and I thought I was out there. You're so far gone I'm going to send out a search party just to pick up your trail."

"Yeah, well it's easy to drift into an idyllic mirage of what life was like, or maybe more accurately, a false idea about what life could be like. But you know, I'm sure all sorts of people look at our lives with envy or even awe. Our wealth and comfort must seem like the garden of Eden to people who struggle to put food on the table."

Richard looked at me and smiled. I knew he was thinking about the conversation that we had begun with our trip and had yet to finish. I saw that it was a conversation that revolved around what it means to be human and what it takes to achieve to the full extent of ones capabilities and what it takes to make the most out of everything God has given us. I suddenly realized the conversation would never be finished. In fact, I saw it was an endless conversation and at first I felt disappointed because I wanted the conversation to arrive at some definite conclusion. I wanted to have everything figured out. I wanted to have an answer that would make every day as perfect as this one. I knew I was the one who was really dreaming.

"You know Richard, from the moment we hit the water back in Ely we have been talking about my business and my life. The trip has been an adventure in many ways but perhaps the most important part of our journey has been this conversation we've yet to finish."

He looked at me as his smile faded into an expression of deep caring. Before he could speak, I held up my hand and said, "I'm not sure what you are about to say but let me share something with you first. I just realized, just this very second, that growing up means being able to accept that things will never be perfect. And, on top of that, I now see that a truly engaged, self-determined human is someone who never stops pursuing the achievement of an ideal model. These people carry on despite knowing their ideal is impossible to attain. It is very clear to me that, just like our trip, the journey through life is where the most profound meaning can be found because it is how you travel through life, not how far you get, that really counts. I know it sounds corny, but I finally realize there is a tremendous amount of wisdom and comfort in an old saying I have always ignored. You know the one, 'It doesn't matter if you win or lose, it's how you play the game". Sure, goals are important, but once achieved what then? Or, what if you set goals and fail? What then? I now understand the only thing we have complete control of is how we carry on... how we live."

"Michael, you certainly got your money's worth on this trip," Richard said. "It's not every day you discover something that will change your life forever."

"Well, I don't know about that. I still have to go

back to a mess, and I still have all my old habits and weaknesses. Things are not going to change overnight you know."

Watching the grin spread over Richard's face I realized the irony in what I had just said. In a split second I had gone back to complaining, blaming and feeling inadequate.

"Don't say it, old habits die hard," I admitted.

"Well, you're making incredible progress and realizing you can't always feel great is part of it. You're beginning to realize the need to accept your fears and frustrations. The more you struggle against them the more power you lend them. If you accept them, you gain power over them, you rule them and you can take charge of your life."

We were standing across the fire from each other. Neither of us had moved while we spoke. A hawk's cry interrupted our concentration and Richard started cleaning up the breakfast dishes. I went up to where we had hidden the other canoe and the outboard engine and dragged each down to the water's edge. Richard brought over the ropes we used to lash the canoes together and the boards to make the transom for the engine.

We were ready to go in less than an hour. As I threw my pack into one of the canoes and climbed into my seat I said, "Hey Richard, before you start that bloody engine, let me ask you a question. I have had the feeling for the last day or so that I'm on the verge of discovering a great truth, some deep meaning for my life. I know it is a major revelation to understand the journey is as important as the goal, but what am I traveling for?"

"Welcome back Grasshopper," he teased. "Hey, I don't have the answer. All I have is a question."

I looked at him, waiting for the question.

"Well, what is it. What's the question already?"

"Do you remember what I told you when I was talking about my first meeting with the Coach? Do you remember the first question he asked me?"

"Yes I do," I said. But I paused. There was no comfort in facing the question because I was afraid I would not have a meaningful answer.

Richard said nothing. He pushed the canoes off the shore, took his seat and reached for the pull-starter on the outboard.

"Wait a minute," I said. "The Coach asked you why you owned your business."

"That's right," Richard said. "Michael, why do you own your business?"

I shook my head and turned away from Richard. He started the engine and we were soon slipping across the water at a speed that seemed unreal after four days of paddling.

The engine and the wind crowded everything else out. I was right back in the man-made world we had so successfully, yet so briefly escaped. I felt I was going back to war and I was wondering why. Why do I own my business? What is the point? It wasn't the money... I had figured that out. It obviously wasn't because I enjoyed the worry or the fear. It had become easier to see all the reasons not to own a business. But, what was it that kept me coming back? What could possibly sustain me and help me take everything to the next level and beyond? Why did I own my business?

What was the meaning of my journey?

The wind and the water were all I was aware of. The drone of the engine faded as I fell deeper and deeper into my thoughts.

Our trip across the bottom of the lake and then down the river to Shagawa Lake took two hours. The time slipped by quickly as if it were keeping pace with our high speed of travel. As we approached Schaefer Bay and the outfitter's marina, I wished we could turn the canoe around and head back into the wilderness. I envied Helen, the root beer lady, for her simple life.

As we pulled into the dock, Moose came striding down from his office.

"Well, you fellows look like you could use a hot shower and a cup of coffee. It's great to see you back safe and sound. How was your trip?"

Richard reached up to take Moose's hand and climbed out of the canoe.

"Oof, I'm stiff from just sitting here for so long," he said as he looked at me with a big grin, "You were right all along Michael, paddling sure beats this bloody outboard."

We unloaded our gear and went up to the office. After settling our bill, Moose showed us into a modest change room with three shower stalls.

"There are fresh towels in the cabinet and plenty of hot water because you're the first folks to come back today."

The shower felt great after days of washing with cold lake water. I stood for a few minutes letting the hot water run through my hair. During the last hours of our trip, while being pushed along by the outboard, it felt like the noise and speed were erasing the wilderness and along with it, the feeling I had that I was on the verge of discovering a great truth.

As we drove to the airstrip, Richard told Moose about our trip. Moose was particularly impressed by our encounter with the bear.

"That sort of thing rarely happens. When canoeists encounter a bear, it's usually from a distance. If one does come into a camp, they are most often the young males who are more curious than anything."

He craned his neck around to look at me and said, "You did OK. I hope you don't go around telling everyone not to come here because the place is full of renegade bears who like to wake up sleeping campers."

"Don't worry, the way things turned out, I consider the bear to be an added bonus, it's like we won a prize for being the one millionth customer."

Moose and Richard laughed and I smiled knowing I would tell that story many times throughout my life.

That stupid bear, the root beer lady, the entire trip were now a permanent part of my life and it made me feel happy and content knowing I could look forward to sharing what happened and what I had learned with my family, friends, and even my goofy brother in law.

We loaded our gear into the plane, said goodbye to Moose, and climbed aboard. Richard instantly transformed from the relaxed loosey-goosey guy who had been teasing me for the past five days into a focused master. He ran through the pre-flight checklist like a drill sergeant, started the engine, taxied to the end of the runway and pulled the throttle wide open. We were just at take off speed when we passed Moose who was standing next to his truck and waving. I waved back as we lifted off. We gained altitude and then Richard turned the plane for home. As it banked, I could see the marina, the bay, and town of Ely pass below. I wondered if I would ever see this place again.

Richard spoke with air traffic control and then turned to look at me as if to invite me to say something. My feelings were so mixed and so powerful, I wasn't ready to restart our conversation. I couldn't come up with an answer to the question of why I owned my business. The answer felt so close, the harder I reached for it, the further it moved away. It was maddening. It was exhausting.

I found myself standing in Richard's office, near a

bookcase, off to one side. Richard was working at his desk and just finishing a telephone conversation.

"That's perfect, I really think I can help you," he said, gently placing the receiver in its cradle. He turned and smiled at me. I knew something wasn't quite right as he stood to greet me; the way he was silhouetted by bright sunshine streaming through the large window behind him seemed too perfect, too intense. An airplane was flying by, the roar of its engine intensifying as Richard came towards me and said, "That was one of the greatest people I've ever known and I am absolutely thrilled to be able to help him."

My head snapped backwards as I awoke from a deep sleep.

"Whoa, Michael, be careful you'll hurt yourself," Richard said over the roar of the airplane engine.

Squinting into the sun, I looked at him and saw concern in his eyes. I realized he truly cared for me. Not just as someone to chum around with, but deeply and completely. He cared for me as a human being. And then it hit me; practically everything he has ever done with me has, in one way or another, been good for me. He has made a real difference in my life and never more so than during this trip.

"Richard, I have the answer."

"What? What was the question?"

I smiled at his feigned artlessness. "I own my business so that I can help people," I said quietly.

"What? Speak up a bit, I can't hear you."

"I own my business so that I can make a real difference in other people's lives. That's why I am in business," I shouted.

"I knew that," Richard said, smiling as broadly as I have ever seen him smile.

"Oh, you did, did you? Well, thanks a lot for stringing me along. This is completely awesome. It is so simple, yet it is really what I am all about. I help people."

"Michael, you have just discovered the deepest meaning of all. The opportunity to help people and make a real difference in their lives is what gives you, and me, true purpose. It is how we are relevant and why we are here. It is what God intended for us."

Richard was interrupted by air traffic control and began to make preparations for landing. I sat in my seat and felt a great weight lift from my shoulders, from my entire being. It was as if the sun were shining inside of me driving away my fears, my guilt, my doubts and my resentment. I had the answer.

After landing the plane, Richard and I loaded our gear into his Land Rover and made the short drive to his acreage. Along the way I talked about how I could hardly wait to get back to work and take a fresh look at everything I was doing. I told him I wanted to look at everything I was doing and put it into context of how it helps other people.

As we pulled into Richard's driveway he said

he wanted to ask me three more questions before I left for home.

"Three more questions! What are you trying to do to me? I just spent five days answering one question and now you want me to take on three more?"

"Relax Grasshopper," Richard said, "These questions are ones you can answer later. I just need you to consider them so you can make the most out of your newly discovered purpose and meaning."

"Sounds a little ominous. Well, what are they?"

"The first one is 'Who do you really care about?'"

"Do you mean at work, at home? Which 'who' are you referring to?"

"I know you care about your family, and your best friends," Richard said winking at me. "But specifically, I want you to figure out who you really care about relative to your business. I want you to define the type of client you are most passionate about helping. And, I want you to do the same with your team... your employees and managers."

"How do I do that?"

"That's easy, just list the characteristics they need to possess. Choose the characteristics that are most important to you; the ones that make them ideal for you."

"OK, what's the next question?"

"Well, that is the next question."

"What do you mean?"

"I mean, the next question is, 'What characteristics do ideal clients and team members possess?'"

"OK, I think I've got it. What's the third question?"

"This is a big one. What do you do to pay your ideal clients and employees back for bringing their ideal characteristics to you?"

"Huh, what do you mean 'pay them back'?"

"Well, I mean if you are going to demand these characteristics from others – and I am telling you to demand these characteristics from everyone you work for and with – what specific tools, methods, wisdom, capabilities and other resources do you bring to the table to help them make the most of who they are?"

I sat there with my mouth open, just staring at Richard. I was incredibly excited about getting started and he had just given me a road map for redefining everything about my business. I saw that if I could acknowledge, protect, and enhance the very best in my clients and employees, I would be able to build a business that truly made a difference to everyone who came into its reach.

"Richard, part of me wants to turn around, fly back to Ely, and take another week to figure all this out. But most of all, I want to go home and hug my wife and kids. I am back and I am better than ever. I'll let you know how things are going in a couple of weeks. Who knows, by then I may need your help more than ever."

"Michael, I am very proud of you," Richard said.

I got out of the Land Rover, unloaded my bag and put it in my car. Richard came around the vehicle and we shook hands. I got into my car and as I drove through the dappled light of his driveway, I looked at Richard in my rearview mirror. He waved once, turned and walked towards his house.

AUTHOR'S NOTE

Our time spent living is precious. I have learned that in order to be the best you can be, you need to be intentional about how you use your energy and your passion. Choosing the right type of people to help is absolutely essential.

> CHAPTER **WORKSHEETS**

Worksheet #11: The Ideal Client Exercises

1. The Ideal Client Conversation

Step #1: List all of the characteristics that make a client ideal

- _____
- _____
- _____
- _____

- _____
- _____
- _____
- _____

Step #2: Describe the specific things you do to Acknowledge, Protect, and Enhance each one of these characteristics.

- _____
- _____
- _____
- _____

- _____
- _____
- _____
- _____

2. The Continuous Improvement Questions

- What are you doing that is great for your clients?
- What are you doing that you need to improve?
- What do you think your company is doing that is great and needs to keep doing?
- What is your company doing that you need to improve?

Answering these questions will always help you decide what you need to do next.

Dreams pass into the reality of action. From the actions stems the dream again; and this interdependence produces the highest form of living.
Anais Nin

ABOUT THE AUTHORS

Donald F. Hadley
President of FFG Companies, Inc.

Donald F. Hadley, CFP®, ChFC, MSM, is the fifth generation of his family to be in small business and has spent the last 23 years coaching passionate business owners on making their mark. As a business owner, he brings practical "in the trenches" methods and tools for dealing with issues that you face today.

The recipient of several degrees and certifications, Don holds a B.A. Cum Laude in Business Management from North Carolina State University in Raleigh, North Carolina; a CFP® (Certified Financial Planner™) from the College of Financial Planning in Denver, Colorado; a MSM (Master of Science in Management), CLU (Chartered Life Underwriter) and ChFC (Chartered Financial Consultant) from the American College in Bryn Mawr, Pennsylvania. Memberships include the Estate Planning Council, FPA (Financial Planning Association), Omicron Delta Epsilon (an honor society in Economics), Sigma Chi Fraternity, the IMA (Institute of Management Accountants), BSF and YPO.

As an educator at heart, Don speaks on a variety

of topics as well as facilitating workshops. He writes financial advisory articles and is published in trade association magazines and newsletters across the United States.

Don is also an Eagle Scout, a model shipbuilder and a world traveler having been to: Alaska, Australia, Canada, the Caribbean, England, France, Italy, Korea, Mexico, Portugal, Thailand, Morocco, the Netherlands and Greece. Don is married with six children and lives in North Carolina.

Curtis Verstraete,
President BIG Incorporated

Curtis is a motivational marketing coach who has helped
hundreds of advisors, business owners, and entrepreneurs achieve breakthroughs
in their business.

He helps people take a new look at their capabilities, expertise and resources to discover untapped
opportunities and assets. His greatest ability is turning unrecognized and under valued intellectual
property into money making processes, programs,
and products.

He also plays the role of a marketing architect in
helping his clients develop unique marketing strategies and plans.

He is a speaker, accomplished seminar host, and
writer.

Prior to founding BIG Incorporated in 1994, Curtis
owned and operated three other businesses including a weekly newspaper, a direct sales company and a
marketing production company.